STORMPROOF
YOUR BOAT

STORMPROOF
YOUR BOAT

THE COMPLETE GUIDE
TO BATTENING DOWN
WHEN STORMS THREATEN

WILLIAM BURR

International Marine / McGraw-Hill

CAMDEN, MAINE • NEW YORK • CHICAGO • SAN FRANCISCO • LISBON • LONDON • MADRID
• MEXICO CITY • MILAN • NEW DELHI • SAN JUAN • SEOUL • SINGAPORE • SYDNEY • TORONTO

The McGraw·Hill Companies

1 2 3 4 5 6 7 8 9 DOC DOC 0 9 8 7 6

Library of Congress Cataloging-in-Publication Data
Burr, William M.
    Stormproof your boat : the complete guide to battening down when storms threaten / William Burr.
        p.   cm.
    Includes index.
    ISBN 0-07-146283-X (pbk. : alk. paper)
1. Boatyards—Safety measures. 2. Boats and boating—Protection. 3. Boats and boating—Storage. 4. Storms—Safety measures. 5. Boating accidents—Prevention. 6. Heavy weather seamanship. I. Title.
    VM321.5B87 2006
    623.8′6—dc22   2006006492

Questions regarding the content of this book should be addressed to
International Marine
P.O. Box 220
Camden, ME 04843
www.internationalmarine.com

Questions regarding the ordering of this book should be addressed to
The McGraw-Hill Companies
Customer Service Department
P.O. Box 547
Blacklick, OH 43004
Retail customers: 1-800-262-4729
Bookstores: 1-800-722-4726

Photographs courtesy the author unless otherwise noted.
Illustrations by Ben White unless otherwise noted.

Note: Suggestions and ideas relating to preparing a boat for a severe storm are based on information gained from numerous reliable sources. In using any of the ideas suggested in this book, the reader releases the author, publisher, and distributor from liability for any loss or injury, including death, allegedly caused, in whole or in part, by relying on information contained in this book.

To Loretta, my inspiration.

Red sky at night, sailor's delight; Red sky
at morning, sailor take warning.

—ANONYMOUS WEATHER SAYING

Contents

Acknowledgments

With considerable humility, the author wishes to thank the real weather experts: Bill Gray, Stan Goldberg, Ed Rappaport, Kevin Trenberth, and Mary Finley-Jones. Also, thanks to those who have learned so much the hard way: Migael Scherer, Mike Keyworth, Phil Jarrell, Larry and Mary Bramlett, Fran and Shirley McGoldrick, Mark Griffis, Dave Robertson, Ken Rohlman, Darren Anderson, and Michael Smith. At International Marine, thanks to Jon Eaton and Bob Holtzman for their invaluable advice and their patience.

Introduction

Stormproof Your Boat is not about survival at sea, a subject that has been studied intensively and written about extensively. This book is about preparedness, about keeping your boat safe whether it's in a slip, on a mooring, at anchor, in dry-stack storage, or on a trailer behind your home. It begins by explaining the threat: the causes and effects of hurricanes, tornadoes, thunderstorms, and sudden summer squalls. It describes how to prepare yourself and your boat against the effects of storm surge, severe wind, torrential rain, and inland flooding, discussing the strategies that work best and the types of locations that provide the most safety. It points to the many media sources that can help you as a boatowner follow the progress of incoming bad weather. It also tells true stories of owners who have lost their boats to storms and of those who won their battles with the elements. Step by step, *Stormproof Your Boat* helps you prepare efficiently and confidently to overcome Mother Nature's worst.

A boat is a serious investment, and its storm survival is solely in its owner's hands. No one wants his vessel damaged or destroyed, but most owners don't know the best ways to prepare their boat to ride out a violent storm. Many good ideas float around the yacht yard regarding what worked during the last storm—along with some not-so-good ideas that come from anecdotal information, "received wisdom," and outright speculation passing as knowledge. These ideas should be considered, but critically.

Probably the only positive side effect from all the storms that have buffeted America's coastlines and inland waters is the tremendous wealth of information that has been gained—data that have been analyzed intensively by professional, industry, and government sources to determine effective defensive strategies. In this book, I have endeavored to bring together the best of these suggestions in illustrations, photographs, and text that are interesting to read and easy to understand.

In recent years, weather forecasting has progressed, making storm prediction more of a science and less of the inefficient art form that it was in the past. No longer do major storms blindside everyone, such as the hurricane of 1938 that slammed into New England without warning. Even in the recent past, hurricane forecasts were only reliable a day in advance. While the prediction of hurricane tracks has improved, it is still far from infallible; we may not know exactly where, but we do know that a hurricane is coming, as much as 5 days in advance. We have time to prepare. No longer do we have the excuse of being surprised.

The only problems left are the boatowner's complacency and lack of knowledge about what works in a particular situation. Choosing the right location for a boat's storm shelter and preparing it properly can make all the difference in reducing storm damage. It has been estimated that of all the boats severely damaged or destroyed in past storms, almost half received little or no protective measures from their owners. Boats that had the least damage weren't just lucky; they had owners who had learned how to interpret coming storms, and who made sound preparations accordingly.

Rarely has there been a subject that touches as many boatowners as storm-damage prevention. It is of interest to those who have made boating a way of life as well as to newcomers. It affects weekenders who relax by trolling for dinner in their 20-footers and commercial fishermen alike. It haunts megayacht owners as much as daysailors.

As a storm approaches, each of these boatowners will sit in front of his or her TV, computer, radio, or newspaper with growing apprehension. In each of their minds is the question, "Will my boat be destroyed or damaged beyond repair?"

Those owners who have dealt with storms year after year have learned how to protect their boats by trial and error, and you will read some of their stories. But, as you will soon see, few storms are exactly alike; probably no two come from the same direction, have the same intensity, hit at the same state of tide, have the same rate of rainfall, etc. There is always a surprise waiting for us, even though we think we have seen it all before. Just look at the devastation wrought by Hurricane Katrina in New Orleans in 2005—the city flooded *after* the storm had passed over it.

Then there are those people who are new to boating and who have no idea of the demons lurking out there—people who have only recently made their first investment in a beloved craft and who are learning from the bottom up.

But the past has shown that both experienced boaters and newcomers are potential victims of every storm.

Storms are infamous for the capriciousness with which they "decide" where and upon what they will inflict their damage. Out of a dozen boats at anchor, six might break loose and be destroyed on the rocks, while the other six ride out the hurricane virtually unscathed. In a marina with rows of dry-stack storage, one or two stacks may fall while the others remain as solid as the day they were built. Storm surge may lift a dock off its pilings on the east side of a marina, releasing all its boats to the mercy of the storm, while the docks on the west side hold solid. Unpredictable? Illogical? Random? How can we predict which boats will suffer and which will survive?

The answer is obvious: there is no way to be absolutely certain your boat will survive a severe storm for the simple reason that the *localized* effects of a storm are not as predictable as its general path. These days, weather reports give quite accurate timing to the broad swath of a coming storm, but they cannot predict precisely what will happen at your marina or at your slip.

While there is little you can do about the random nature of a storm's effects, there is a great deal you can do to make sure your boat isn't the one that breaks loose from its mooring and goes tearing across the harbor.

Chance is always out there and no matter how well you prepare your boat for a coming storm, it can still become one of the unlucky ones. No book, and no amount of preparation, can make your boat invulnerable to bad luck.

This book is for boatowners whose boat has not yet been given every chance to survive: the boat that might be wrecked because its anchor rode is chafed, the boat with brand-new lines that are not protected with chafing gear, the boat that is thoughtlessly left on its trailer and not tied down, or the boat tied to poorly mounted dock cleats with short lengths of thin line. These and other potential problems are all preventable with a little forethought and action.

I hope that this book will supply the information that you, as a boatowner, need in order to act in a timely, efficient, and effective manner. Storms will not go away. In fact, we have been advised that they are becoming more frequent and more severe. All we can do is prepare better. By implementing the proven strategies in this book, you'll go a long way toward having an undamaged boat when the weather clears and the violence of the storm is over. We can't prevent bad luck, but we can shift the odds in our favor.

The Nature of the Beast

In early September of 2004, having weathered Hurricane Charley and Hurricane Frances successfully, Alex Covil decided to leave Miami and visit his brother in the North Carolina mountains rather than spend the rest of the summer fussing and worrying about his boat at the marina. Only 3 weeks remained in the hurricane season, and a third hurricane striking the same area in the same year was unheard of. He knew he was taking a risk but decided to go. Florida had been hit hard, but his boat had survived the previous storms without incident, and he expected the same results if another hurricane popped up. After all, what more could he do about it? Extra-long lines and additional fenders had worked just fine in the two previous hurricanes, and he left these precautionary measures in place when he left town.

While Alex was in the mountains, hurricane number three—Jeanne—whistled toward his little marina. The early wind bands gusted to 108 miles per hour and parted his boat's dock lines, which had been badly chafed in the previous storms. Free of its confinement, Alex's boat spent the next hour banging into boat after boat as it charged along the slips and out into the channel, where it sank in 12 feet of water.

Alex's boat was a victim of his complacency. Even though he was one of the few who had educated himself on storm preparedness, he failed to repeat his preparations after the earlier hurricanes. He thought he had taken all the precautions necessary, but he failed to go back and check his lines for chafe after the earlier storms. He failed to talk with his neighbors or the marina staff about looking after his boat while he was away. A little forethought and preventive action might have saved his boat, but instead he let down his guard. Alex's story is one of thousands where a boat would have suffered little damage if it had been properly attended to.

THE DANGER OF COMPLACENCY

No matter where a boat is kept—at anchor, on a mooring, in a slip, or even "safely" on land—there is a high probability that it will be severely damaged or destroyed by a severe storm *if it is inadequately prepared.*

Hurricane Katrina made a mess of this New Orleans marina in 2005. Notice how the docks remained intact; many of the damaged boats might have survived had their owners made better preparations. (Courtesy FEMA)

Because of the havoc caused by recent hurricanes along our coastlines and inland, boatowners throughout the United States are more concerned than ever about protecting their boats from storm-related damage. Television, radio, and Internet coverage bring vivid descriptions of devastation into every household where boatowners anxiously wait out storms. In many cases, the apprehension increases after the storm passes when flooding, power outages, police cordons, and communication system failures keep owners out of the devastated areas, unable to learn the fate of their boats. Safe reentry to boatyards and marinas may not be possible until days or even weeks after the storm.

Many residents along the East and Gulf coasts fail to take even simple steps to protect themselves and their homes, much less their boats, from hurricanes. One 2005 poll by Mason-Dixon Polling and Research suggested that one in four people do nothing to prepare for a storm, even after a watch or warning has been issued. The poll also found that one in four residents believe they can successfully evacuate flood-prone areas in as little as 30 minutes to an hour before a hurricane makes landfall. Almost half (47 percent) make no contingency disaster plan, and 54 percent think that crisscrossing their windows with masking tape will prevent them from shattering. (For years, this latter practice has been known to be a myth.) Ninety-six percent are unaware that the structural element most likely to fail first in a hurricane is a garage door.

After the 2005 hurricane season, which included the devastating storms Katrina and Rita, more people should now be aware that a 30-minute evacuation plan is so inadequate as to be absurd. Unfortunately, memory is short-lived, and in all likelihood, this valuable lesson will be largely forgotten in a year's time.

Although the polling sample was from the general population and not just the boating sector, the same casual and ill-prepared approach to an upcoming storm is apparent among many boatowners.

And to make matters worse, climate and storm experts now predict that the next two decades will bring a major increase in the frequency and severity of damaging storms. Because of this increasing threat, concerned boatowners need to learn the best ways to protect their vessels from the effects of severe storms.

TYPES OF STORMS

Other than winter ice and snow or a once-a-decade astronomical high tide, nature rarely threatens boats in harbors or on land—except when major storms come calling. These are of several types: hurricanes, thunderstorms and line squalls, tornadoes, and regional winds.

Hurricanes should be considered the most dangerous storms because they are probably nature's largest expenditure of raw energy. These superstorms threaten almost all U.S. coastlines, except the Northwest and Great Lakes, and impact huge geographic strike areas, often far into the interior. Thunderstorms, line squalls, tornadoes, and local wind phenomena like California's Santa Ana winds can be devastating but are generally short lived and localized. The storm surges and high seas common in hurricanes are not usually present in these localized storms. But wind gusts of 50 to 70 miles per hour with driving rain are not uncommon in thunderstorms and line squalls and should not be taken lightly.

A considerable amount of hurricane prediction is based on history as well as on current weather conditions, and, unfortunately, humankind has not been keeping reliable weather records for very long. As Christopher C. Burt observes in his book, *Extreme Weather* (Norton, 2004):

"In the United States, weather records have been maintained by the official weather services since about 1870. In the 50 preceding years, records were kept intermittently by individuals and by some institutions, including the Smithsonian Institution. [The figures we have] represent only a fraction of human experience with weather."

The bottom line is that 135 years or so of accurate weather records don't give forecasters much data to work with. While history has shown us how *far* a hurricane

Although the accuracy of hurricane track predictions has improved greatly in recent years, there is still much uncertainty regarding the path of even a single storm—all the more reason for proper preparations when any storm approaches your boat. (Courtesy NOAA)

might advance in 5 days, it hasn't revealed enough clear patterns for us to predict a hurricane's *direction* with the same accuracy.

In contrast to hurricane advisories, thunderstorms are so localized that weather stations often have less than an hour in which to issue a warning. If your weather station is like mine, a typical forecast during the summer months is, "Hot and humid, with a chance of a late afternoon thunderstorm." When is the last time you rushed down to the slip to add extra lines after hearing a warning like that?

Summer thunderstorms and late afternoon squalls are so common in places like the Chesapeake Bay that boaters have learned to expect them on an almost daily basis. But where thunderstorms can't be so confidently anticipated, the very unexpectedness of their arrival makes them more dangerous.

Tornadoes are unique phenomena. They are intense atmospheric vacuum cleaners with winds that can reach speeds of 200 miles per hour and more. But although their destructive force is almost total where they hit, they generally touch down on such a small area that the chance of your boat being damaged is quite low compared to storms that cover a large area and last a long time.

Most of us think tornadoes strike only in the Great Plains states. But tornadoes are also spawned by hurricanes and can occur anywhere these larger storms appear. After

Lightning is just one of the dangers of thunderstorms. The frequency of thunderstorms can lead boatowners to be complacent about their potentially damaging winds. (Courtesy NOAA)

a hurricane hits land, its destructive force is generally reduced by the loss of the warm water that fuels it. However, the summer of 2004 was a perfect example of the devastation that can be caused by hurricane-spawned tornadoes well outside "Tornado Alley," when twisters from Hurricanes Ivan and Jeanne struck deep in the *interior* of Florida and North Carolina.

One of the areas of the country least affected by severe weather is the Pacific Northwest. Boatowners there generally keep their boats in the water year-round due to the mild temperatures. But even there, bad weather happens. Storms come from low-pressure systems out of the Pacific Ocean and follow the mountainous coast north or south. Often two winds will meet in a convergence zone, or storm winds will oppose strong currents. Either condition can cause steep or confused waves that intensify where waterways narrow. So when someone says the Northwest has no bad weather, don't believe it. No matter where you are, there are weather conditions to understand and be concerned about.

This book addresses all these storms, but the greatest emphasis is on hurricanes, with their quadruple whammy of high winds, storm surge, heavy surf, and torrential rain.

Although you can take measures to secure small boats on land, little can stand up to a direct hit by a powerful tornado. (Courtesy NOAA)

These are the storms that cause the most widespread damage to boats, but thankfully, they are also the storms boatowners can do the most to protect their boats from. Because of their history of severity, their effects are well documented. Because they take days to develop, they get our attention rather than indifference. We have both time and proven methods to prepare our boats to better withstand what nature can throw at them.

To better know what you are up against, the following chapters describe each type of storm in more detail: what causes it, where it comes from, why it strikes where it does, how its intensity is described, and where it is most prevalent. When we know how big and how dangerous a storm can be, we won't just worry our way through the tempest, but will head out to the slip or anchorage and put the boat in its best defensive position. Then we can go home, hunker down, and wait out the storm with a much higher level of confidence that all will be well.

Hurricanes

A hurricane is a large rotating storm of tropical origin that forms over warm ocean water, ranges from 60 to 1,000 miles in diameter, and has winds of at least 74 miles per hour. Hurricanes are called different names, depending on where they occur. You've probably heard of severe storms elsewhere in the world and didn't realize that they were actually hurricanes by another name:

- **Hurricane:** storms in the North Atlantic Ocean, the Northeast Pacific Ocean east of the dateline, and the South Pacific Ocean east of 160 degrees east.
- **Typhoon:** storms in the Northwest Pacific Ocean west of the dateline.
- **Severe tropical cyclone:** storms in the Southwest Pacific Ocean west of 160 degrees east and the Southeast Indian Ocean east of 90 degrees east.
- **Severe cyclonic storm:** storms in the North Indian Ocean.
- **Tropical cyclone:** storms in the Southwest Indian Ocean.

No matter what the storm's name or where it occurs, we North Americans are most interested in the behavior of hurricanes in the North Atlantic (including the Caribbean Sea and the Gulf of Mexico) and in the Pacific Ocean off the coasts of California and Mexico. Though it is probably of little comfort, only 12 percent of the world's tropical cyclones occur in these places. Approximately 96 tropical cyclones are reported worldwide annually, and they can come from three of the four oceans and in both hemispheres. The Indian Ocean has the most activity.

Hurricanes heading toward the U.S. East Coast usually move at about 10 to 20 miles per hour from east to west and last a few days to a couple of weeks. Spiraling counterclockwise around a relatively calm center called the eye, a hurricane's winds can produce gusts of 200 miles per hour as far out as 30 miles from the eye. Even 200 miles in advance of a hurricane, winds can exceed 40 miles per hour.

HURRICANE FORMATION AND DEVELOPMENT

Hurricanes are incredibly complex mechanisms, requiring a large number of variables to fall into place "just so." If any of these variables is lacking or its value falls outside certain parameters, the storm may remain a tropical disturbance or storm, or it may dissipate altogether.

The three basic requirements of hurricane formation are:

1. *An energy source:* the heat stored in the warm waters of tropical oceans. The water temperature must be approximately 80°F or higher, which occurs predictably during the summer months. This warm water must extend to a depth of approximately 150 feet to keep heat energy available to the storm system even after the wind begins churning up the ocean.

2. *A vertical transport mechanism:* a series of thunderstorms that lifts evaporated water high into the atmosphere, where moisture and heat are released. Just one thunderstorm isn't sufficient; there must be considerable thunderstorm activity to provide sufficient vertical transport. Additionally, for the transport to remain vertical, there must be low *wind shear*, which is the difference between the speed and direction of winds at high and low levels of the atmosphere. If surface winds are light and winds in the upper atmosphere are strong or moving in different directions, the resulting shear will tear the top off the storm, and it will collapse.

3. *A cyclonic (swirling) wind pattern:* winds must converge, bringing the thunderstorms closer together at least 500 miles from the equator, so that the Coriolis force can set the system turning counterclockwise in the northern hemisphere or clockwise in the southern hemisphere. The *Coriolis force* is an apparent force that, as a result of the earth's rotation, deflects moving objects—such as air currents—to the right in the northern hemisphere and to the left in the southern hemisphere. Its strength varies with distance from the equator, where the force is zero, to the poles, where it's at its maximum. If depressions are too close to the equator, they will not have enough rotational energy to develop into tropical cyclones.

A hurricane's life begins when a cluster of strong thunderstorms moves across a warm ocean. At this stage, the phenomenon is called a tropical disturbance or a tropical wave. Most North Atlantic hurricanes have their birth in converging winds that move out over the ocean from western Africa in an easterly wave (for more on easterly waves, see page 12).

As with all thunderstorms, a tropical wave is an area of low atmospheric pressure, which draws winds in from surrounding areas of higher pressure. Evaporation at the ocean's surface puts moisture into the atmosphere. As the warm, moist air rises, the

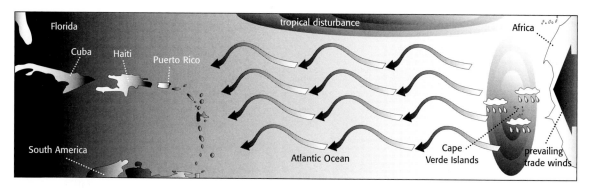

Easterly waves—a type of tropical disturbance—arise from instability in the prevailing trade winds. During hurricane season, a wave forms every 3 or 4 days in the North Atlantic, many of them over the Cape Verde Islands. If conditions are right, converging winds trigger thunderstorms, and possibly the convection and rotation necessary for tropical storm development.

water vapor condenses, releasing heat energy and feeding the thunderstorms. The surrounding air warms further and rises, reducing atmospheric pressure even more. A positive feedback loop is created: the more evaporation, the greater the release of heat energy in the upper atmosphere, creating even lower air pressure and stronger winds that bring in moist air from surrounding areas, resulting in more evaporation.

If the storm is at least 8 degrees north or south of the equator, the Coriolis force sets the system spinning, and an eye begins to form. (Although the Coriolis force increases with distance from the equator, hurricanes rarely form above 20 degrees latitude, because the ocean water there is not warm enough.) The eye is a central cylinder of calm winds and no clouds, surrounded by a swirling mass of high storm winds. It can range from 5 to over 120 miles in diameter, and its formation is evidence of a well-organized storm that stands a good chance of becoming a hurricane. The perimeter of the eye is the eyewall, which has the highest surface winds in the tropical cyclone. While the air in the eye is slowly sinking, the air at the eyewall is rapidly rising (see illustration next page).

Hurricanes also have long narrow rainbands swirling around the eye (see photo page 11), oriented by the wind (counterclockwise in the northern hemisphere). These bands move toward the center, narrowing and encircling it until the eye and eyewall form.

As warm air continues to rise, atmospheric pressure eventually has to build up somewhere. If wind shear is low, air pressure begins to increase in the high atmosphere directly above the thunderstorms. This high-pressure cap forces additional rising air to move out in all directions away from the center of the storm system. It then cools, descends to ocean level outside of the low-pressure core, picks up more moisture, moves back in toward the low-pressure center of the swirling storm system, and rises again—releasing yet more moisture and heat into the atmosphere.

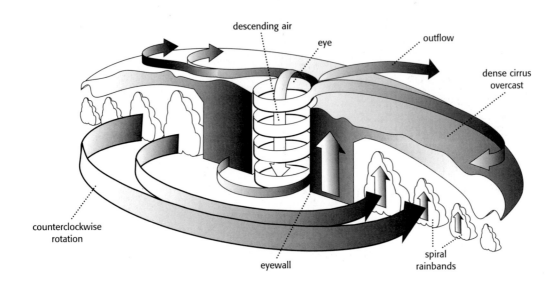

Many variables have to fall into place "just so" for the amazingly complex structure of a hurricane to form.

If nothing interferes with these horizontal and vertical circulation patterns, and the storm remains over warm water that can continually provide energy, the surface wind speeds will continue to increase, and the system will achieve hurricane status. Alter any one of these conditions, and the storm will die.

Additional Factors to Watch

Satellite images have allowed us to watch storms and their progress, almost from the moment of their birth (see Chapter 6 for website resources). They go through growth spurts, like a child. After observing many of them, you begin to recognize the telltale signs of strengthening: speed of forward travel, wind force, direction, eye formation, and spiral bands. You become adept at picking up clues as to whether the necessary conditions, such as sea temperature, exist for further strengthening. Though these pieces of information don't tell you exactly where or when the storm will strike, they bring you close to the rapid development of the storm.

Time of Year

Because high ocean temperatures are an essential precondition, the time of the year is an important factor. The official hurricane season lasts from June through November in the northern hemisphere, with September 10 as the historical peak. Tropical storms can develop even into December, although at that time of year they rarely result in full-fledged hurricanes.

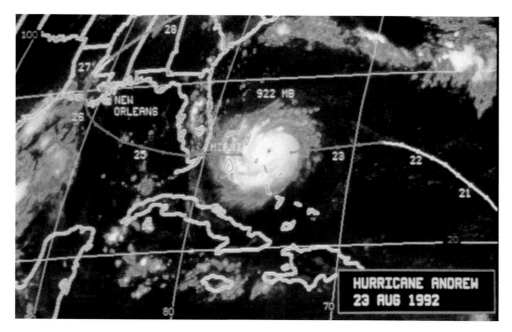

Hurricane Andrew's eye and its swirling rainbands are clearly visible in this satellite photograph. The faint line shows the eye's past and projected tracks (lower right and upper left, respectively). (Courtesy NOAA)

El Niño

In "normal years" the Pacific trade winds blow strongly enough to push the surface warm water layer westward, causing a buildup of warm water in the western Pacific. Cold deep-ocean water wells up along the South American coast to replace the water that is pushed westward, which results in warmer ocean surface temperatures in the Eastern Pacific. During El Niño years the trade winds are lighter than normal, and cannot power the "normal" westward water currents, which also decline, so the water in the eastern Pacific becomes warmer than normal. This causes a reduction in the cold upwelling currents and abnormally high rainfall along the west coast of the Americas.

The phenomenon, which lasts for a year or more, occurs at irregular intervals of 2 to 7 years and has a significant effect on weather worldwide. Researchers have determined that there are fewer North Atlantic hurricanes during El Niño years because of increased wind shear in the atmosphere over the Caribbean and the Atlantic. When wind shear is strong, the storms become slanted, and the heat that is released by moisture condensing in the atmosphere is dispersed over too large an area to establish a self-reinforcing vertical transport mechanism (see top illustration next page).

The La Niña phenomenon is the reverse—the "normal" patterns are reinforced: trade winds are stronger than usual, moving warm water even farther west. Hurricane frequency and intensity in the North Atlantic both increase.

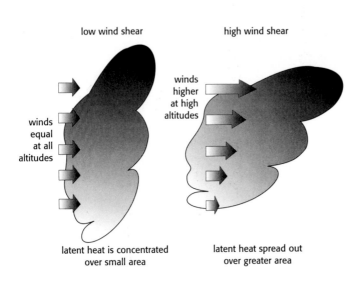

Higher wind shear—as occurs during El Niño years—inhibits hurricane formation by preventing latent heat from stacking up vertically.

Easterly Waves

As mentioned above, in the North Atlantic about 60 percent of hurricanes, including nearly 85 percent of major hurricanes (Category 3 or above), originate from easterly waves. About 60 easterly waves are generated over Africa each year—one every 3 or 4 days during hurricane season. A large percentage of North Atlantic hurricanes begin as disturbances in the vicinity of the Cape Verde Islands off Africa (see illustration page 9) arising from instability of the African easterly jet caused by the contrast between hot air from the Sahara Desert and cooler air along the coast of the Gulf of Guinea. Hurricanes can also pop up almost anywhere along the way, from the trailing ends of cold fronts and, occasionally, from low pressure in the upper atmosphere. By watching for Cape Verde disturbances on world weather resources (see Chapter 6), you can keep track of a large percentage of potential storms in their earliest phases of development.

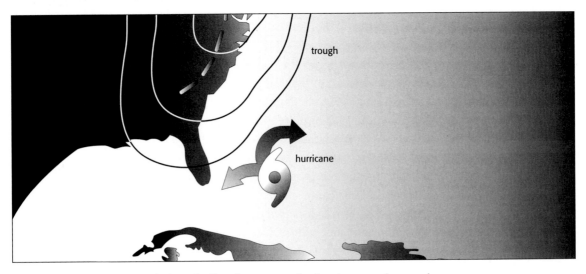

A long-lived trough (or TROF) along the East Coast can push a hurricane north or south.

Poleward Drift

Once over the warm ocean, most storms move toward the west with a slight poleward drift. What is difficult to forecast is whether the tropical cyclone will curve more strongly toward the north and dissipate in the far reaches of the colder North Atlantic, or continue straight ahead, gathering heat energy from the ocean.

Troughs

A trough (TROF, in weather-speak, shown on weather charts as a dashed line) is an elongated area of low pressure where the rising air is often squeezed between two areas of high pressure called ridges. Large weather systems like this can significantly affect a storm's direction. For example, a trough along the East Coast of the United States will often indicate the presence of a ridge that will steer storms to the north well before they approach land (see bottom illustration, opposite).

HURRICANE DAMAGE

Once a storm's sustained winds reach 74 miles per hour, it is considered a full-fledged Category 1 hurricane (sustained winds are determined by averaging wind measurements over a 2-minute period). Hurricane strength is rated by the Saffir-Simpson hurri-

FOR THE COMMITTED STORM WATCHER

The weather website Caribwx (www.caribwx.com) is a favorite of mine and of yachtsmen cruising Caribbean waters. Caribwx president Mary Finley-Jones has written extensively on the key factors of hurricane formation in the tropical Atlantic and the Caribbean. She suggests that serious students of hurricane formation pay attention to the following indices:

- *The amount of rain in the Sahel region of eastern Africa:* more rain indicates more tropical storm development.
- *Sea surface temperatures (SST) in the tropical Atlantic:* higher water temperatures indicate more tropical storm development.
- *El Niño or La Niña conditions:* in El Niño years, a strong, easterly-flowing, upper-level jet stream inhibits tropical storm system development by shearing off the tops of convection clouds. This keeps hurricanes from developing. A warm or strong El Niño condition, therefore, indicates poor potential for tropical development in the Atlantic. However, a La Niña year indicates more tropical storm development in the Atlantic.

  Think of it this way: given a certain amount of energy in the earth's total ocean/atmosphere system, if more of it is in the Pacific, less of it will be available to fuel tropical storm development in the Atlantic.
- *Jet stream location and speed of 200 millibar (mb) winds:* the weaker and farther north upper-level, jet stream winds are at the 200-millibar level, the more tropical storm development will occur. Conversely, strong and more southerly jet stream winds inhibit hurricane development.
- *Surface air pressure in the tropical Atlantic, particularly in the Caribbean Basin:* the lower the air pressure, the better the conditions are for more tropical storm development.
- *A semipermanent, upper-level trough along the U.S. East Coast:* think of a trough as a valley, and a ridge as a hilltop. Though it is a complex relationship, storms tend to follow the higher-air-pressure ridge and are turned away by low-pressure troughs.

cane scale as shown next page. The rankings go up about 20 miles per hour for each category until they reach Category 5 with winds over 156 miles per hour. (The highest recorded wind speeds in a hurricane were over 200 miles per hour—Hurricane Camille, August 1969.) Wind speed is the dominant factor in the scale, but barometric pressure and the height of storm surge also play a role in defining each category.

The Saffir-Simpson Hurricane Scale

CATEGORY	WIND SPEED (MPH/KNOTS)	BAROMETRIC PRESSURE (MB)	STORM SURGE (FEET)	EFFECTS
1	74–95/64–82	980+	3–5	Overall damage is minimal. Light damage to building structures, primarily to unanchored homes, shrubbery, and trees. Also, some coastal road flooding and minor pier damage.
2	96–110/83–95	965–979	6–8	Overall damage is moderate. Some roofing, door, and window damage to buildings. Considerable damage to vegetation, mobile homes, and piers. Coastal and low-lying escape routes flood 2 to 4 hours before arrival of center. Small craft in unprotected anchorages may break moorings.
3	111–130/96–113	945–964	9–12	Overall damage is extensive. Some structural damage to small residences and utility buildings with a minor amount of curtain wall failures. Mobile homes are destroyed. Flooding near the coast destroys smaller structures with larger structures damaged by floating debris. Terrain continuously lower than 5 feet above mean sea level may be flooded inland 8 miles or more.
4	131–155/114–135	920–944	13–18	Overall damage is extreme. More extensive curtain wall failures with some complete roof structure failure on small residences. Major erosion of beaches. Major damage to lower floors of structures near the shore. Terrain continuously lower than 10 feet above mean sea level may be flooded, requiring massive evacuation of residential areas inland as far as 6 miles.
5	156+/136+	< 920	19+	Overall damage is catastrophic. Complete roof failure on many residences and industrial buildings. Some complete building failures with small utility buildings blown over or away. Major damage to lower floors of all structures located less than 15 feet above mean sea level and within 500 yards of the shoreline. Massive evacuation of residential areas on low ground within 5 to 10 miles of the shoreline may be required.

Source: NOAA

Mere speed is a somewhat deceptive measure of a wind's destructive force, however, because when wind speed doubles, its pressure quadruples. And don't be lulled into complacency by thinking that the winds will be strong only when the storm hits shore. Damaging winds will begin well before the hurricane makes landfall. After making landfall a hurricane begins to weaken within hours because the loss of the moisture and heat from the warm ocean water deprives it of its fuel. Many people believe, incorrectly, that it is the friction caused by land that slows the winds and kills the storm. While there is evidence that storm winds are reduced because of the interaction with land, this is not the primary reason for the storm's weakening, and wind gusts can actually grow stronger over land. As the wind passes over topographic features, turbulence increases, bringing faster, higher-altitude winds down to ground level in short bursts.

Another danger, storm surge, is created by the storm's huge area of low barometric pressure, which actually draws the ocean level upward and creates a mound of water approximately 100 miles in diameter and 1 foot higher than normal. As the wind drives this enormous mass of water before it and the surge nears shore, the slope of the sea bottom pushes the water higher and higher until it sweeps ashore like a bulldozer. And on top of that, the wind generates huge waves, raising the maximum water height even farther (see illustrations below and next page).

A typical storm surge can result in a pressure of over 10,000 pounds per square foot. It is this enormous force that causes the most damage when the surge strikes land—followed immediately by widespread flooding.

Upon landfall, the storm still carries huge quantities of moisture that falls as rain. The heaviest rains usually fall to the right of the storm's track in the period from 6

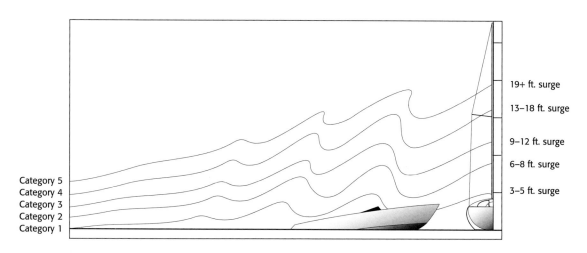

The Saffir-Simpson scale includes storm surge predictions associated with wind speeds. The storm surge is usually the most destructive element of a hurricane.

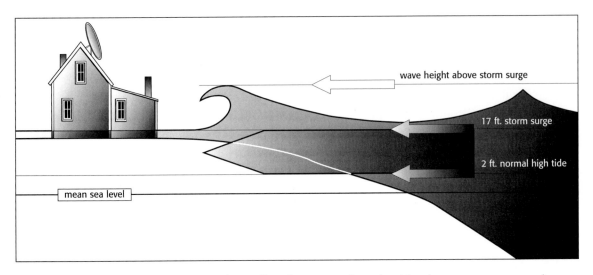

The height of the storm surge above sea level isn't all you have to watch out for. After the storm surge comes ashore, it can pile up even higher—and there will be wind-driven waves on top of that! The illustration shows the devastating effect of a storm surge 17 feet above sea level.

hours before until 6 hours after landfall. The more slowly the storm moves, the longer it has to dump rain over a given area.

Inland flooding can be a major threat when intense, protracted rain falls on communities hundreds of miles inland. When overflowing small creeks flow into larger rivers, flash floods can inundate huge areas. The inability of these natural waterways to handle the excess water means that a heavy rain upstream can produce flooding within a few hours in locales where little rain has fallen, even in a completely dry valley or canyon. As shown in the table opposite, more than half the deaths associated with tropical cyclones in the United States are caused by freshwater inland flooding.

Yet another hurricane-related threat is tornadoes, which form under very particular conditions of atmospheric instability and vertical shear. In conventional tornadoes, like the ones common in the Great Plains, the critical instability typically occurs at altitudes over 20,000 feet. In contrast, the vertical instability of hurricanes over land typically occurs below 10,000 feet. This is a condition that is favorable for the production of small, supercell storms that often spawn tornadoes, although these tend to be smaller and shallower than the ones formed at higher altitudes in Tornado Alley. Hurricane-spawned tornadoes generally occur in the right front quadrant of the hurricane but can occasionally be found elsewhere in the rainbands.

Because these tornadoes are small, they may not look particularly threatening on weather radars. They produce little or no lightning and thunder, move rapidly, and are often obscured by rain. This is the perfect scenario for a boater to be caught unprepared. Any warning comes almost too late to put boat protection plans into

U.S. Tropical Cyclone Deaths, by Cause (1970–1999)	
CAUSE	**PERCENT**
Freshwater flooding	59
Wind	12
Surf	11
Offshore	11
Tornado	4
Storm surge	1
Other causes	2

Source: NOAA

effect. Every boater should be aware of the possibility that tornadoes can follow a hurricane's landfall. See Chapter 3 for more on tornadoes.

THE AREA OF GREATEST DANGER

Because hurricane winds circulate counterclockwise in the northern hemisphere, the wind direction at your boat's storage location will depend on where it is relative to the storm's eye. The worst place to be is just to the right of the eye; for example, to the east of the eye in a north-moving storm. In that upper-right quadrant, the storm's internal, swirling winds are traveling in the same direction as the overall system. The two speeds are additive, so if a storm has internal winds of 95 miles per hour, and the storm system is moving forward at 10 miles per hour, this area will experience winds of 105 miles per hour. Conversely, if your boat is to the left of the eye as the storm moves forward, wind speeds will be lower (95 − 10 = 85 mph) because the internal winds will be moving in the opposite direction to the system (see illustration next page).

High winds are not the only factor that makes the right sector the most dangerous. The higher winds are accompanied by higher wave heights and storm surge and an increased likelihood of tornadoes.

HURRICANE DAMAGE INLAND

Wilkes-Barre, Pennsylvania, sits a hundred miles inland on the upper reaches of the Susquehanna River. It is fortified by huge levees along the river, which sweeps by on its journey through the Pocono Mountains toward the Chesapeake Bay far downstream. In 1972, Hurricane Agnes dumped torrential rains that turned the river into a raging torrent, which overtopped the levees. Water poured into the city, flooding it with 9 feet of silt-laden water. In some places the water reached 18 feet high and lapped at the third story of buildings. Every boat moored on the river was swept away.

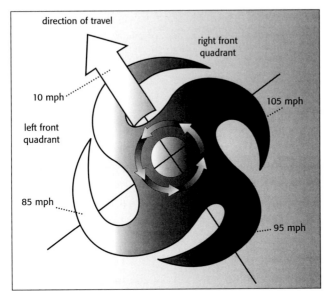

Wind speed is cumulative in a hurricane's right front quadrant because the internal winds are moving in the same direction as the storm's overall direction of travel. In the left front quadrant, wind speeds are less because the winds are moving in the opposite direction to the storm.

Therefore, in a northbound hurricane, the sector to the east of the eye will have the strongest winds, and they will come from the south. The maximum storm surge occurs 10 to 20 miles to the right of the eye, at or near the point of maximum winds. If the storm surge hits shore at the same time as high tide, the combination of surge, high tide, and high winds can be especially deadly.

The left zone, to the eye's west, will have winds coming from the north, and they will be the storm's weakest winds. However, they may still be strong enough to do substantial damage, and to produce the opposite of a storm surge—force water away from shore, creating very low water conditions. Directly in front of the eye, the north zone or leading edge will have winds that last the longest and come mainly from the east—until the eye passes over, after which the area will catch the south zone, or trailing edge, of the storm, with winds coming from the west.

Of course, hurricane prediction is an inexact science, so while you should use the storm's projected course as a guide to the type and extent of preparations you make to protect your boat, always remember the storm might confound the meteorologists and approach from a direction other than that predicted. In general, hurricanes that make a perpendicular approach to land, as is typical in the Gulf Coast, tend to have the smallest amount of forecast error. Conversely, systems that are forecast to run more nearly parallel to the coast, as often happens in the mid-Atlantic region of the United States, tend to have larger track errors.

THREATS TO BOATS AND MARINAS

Now that we know the main causes and risks, let's look at the effects on boat safety as a function of hurricane strength.

Category 1: Winds 74 to 95 mph (64 to 82 kn), storm surge 3 to 5 feet above mean sea level. Coastal road flooding will restrict access to your boat. Minor pier damage may occur. Poorly secured boats may break free.

Category 2: Winds 96 to 110 mph (83 to 95 kn), storm surge 6 to 8 feet above mean sea level. Small craft in unprotected anchorages will probably break moorings.

Some damage will occur to marina roofs and windows, resulting in flying debris that could damage boats stored outside. Some trees will be blown down (particularly those with shallow roots, like many palms), endangering boats stored beneath them. Some coastal evacuation routes may be flooded.

Category 3: Winds 111 to 130 mph (96 to 113 kn), storm surge 9 to 12 feet above mean sea level. Flooding near the coast may destroy smaller structures at marinas. Larger structures may be damaged by battering from floating debris. Substantial flooding extending along rivers and sounds. Because evacuation of low-lying areas is normally required, access to boats may be restricted for many hours before the storm makes landfall.

Category 4: Winds 131 to 155 mph (114 to 135 kn), storm surge 13 to 18 feet above mean sea level. Extensive damage and flooding in low-lying areas. Boats likely to be floated off jack stands in marinas (if they're not blown off). All terrain lower than 10 feet above sea level may be flooded, requiring massive evacuations as much as 6 miles inland. Roof and wall failures will be extensive at marinas and can affect all boats.

Category 5: Winds 156 mph or higher (136+ kn), storm surge 19 feet or more above mean sea level. Extensive damage to all structures and boats located less than 15 feet above sea level. Massive evacuations for residents within 10 miles of the shoreline may restrict post-storm access to marinas for days or weeks.

STORMS OF THE FUTURE

Conditions conducive to hurricane development are changing. Research indicates that hurricane activity waxes and wanes on an alternating cycle, with each phase lasting 25 to 35 years. Between 1928 and 1965, Florida experienced fourteen major hurricane landfalls. Then the cycle shifted, and between 1966 and the early 1990s, only one major hurricane made landfall in Florida (in 1992—but that was a monster called Andrew). The 30-year lull that drew so many millions to live on our coastlines appears to have ended in the 1990s, and we are now in the midst of a new cycle of more intense hurricane activity. More storms, and more violent storms, are expected to make landfall all along the East and Gulf coasts from Maine to Texas.

Ocean circulation patterns appear to cause these alternating phases of high and low hurricane activity. When currents in the Atlantic Ocean are stronger, more major hurricanes develop; when currents are weaker, fewer hurricanes result. Behind it all are changes in the ocean's salinity, which increases when fair weather (low rainfall and sunny skies) leads to accelerated evaporation and less fresh water entering the ocean basin. Lower-salinity waters from the other oceans then flow into the North Atlantic more rapidly than usual, attempting to reach equilibrium. These currents result in warmer surface water temperatures and lower air pressure at sea level—two major factors conducive to the development of hurricanes.

The increasing number of hurricanes in recent years—including Katrina, which damaged marinas throughout the Gulf Coast region, like this one in New Orleans—is associated with global climate change. (Courtesy FEMA)

Satellite measurements also show an increase in water vapor over the oceans worldwide since 1988. The warmer and more abundant moisture furnishes more energy for the storms that fuel developing hurricanes.

And there is some evidence that a warmer earth may bring stronger storms. Kevin Trenberth, head of the Climate Analysis Section at the National Center for Atmospheric Research, reported in an article in the journal *Science* (July 17, 2005) that "Trends in human-influenced environmental changes are now evident in hurricane regions." As he noted in NCAR's October 2004 *Staff Notes Monthly*, "Global climate change, and global warming in particular, create a different background environment in which hurricanes are working. The sea surface temperatures are a little warmer, the whole environment is a bit wetter, there's more humidity, and that's the main fuel for hurricanes."

From the experience of recent storms, it is apparent that many coastal residents were not fully aware of the hurricane risk when they purchased property during the last few decades. Much of the United States coastlines experienced a huge population explosion that coincided with the lull in hurricane activity. This lull gave millions of people a false sense of security, which was shattered in 2004 when a record four hurricanes and one tropical storm hit Florida within a 48-day period, resulting in insurance claims topping $20 billion and an additional $20 billion in uninsured losses.

These photos of devastation in Ocean Springs, Mississippi, were taken a month after Katrina hit. (Courtesy Sea Tow Services International)

(Japan also experienced a record number of storms in 2004.) Fortunately, all four of these hurricanes came ashore in areas that were not densely populated. But the South's luck changed in 2005, when Hurricanes Katrina and Rita caused widespread devastation in Alabama, Louisiana, Mississippi, and Texas.

Hurricane expert Dr. Bill Gray at Colorado State University in his summary of the 2004 season (November 19, 2004) said that the 2004 experience was a "rare anomaly," "unprecedented in terms of historical records going back 130 years," and unlikely to be repeated anytime soon. In other words, while scientists may notice a statistical increase in hurricane activity, the bottom line is—don't panic, but be prepared.

3 Tornadoes, Thunderstorms, Nor'easters, and Regional Winds

While hurricanes cause the most widespread destruction, other more localized events can just as easily destroy your boat. Some, like thunderstorms, can happen virtually at any time, and will probably affect your boat at some point; your best defense is a general policy of keeping your boat and its contents well maintained and well secured. Others, like tornadoes, occur more seasonally and cover far smaller footprints. While your chances of being hit by a tornado are considerably less, the damage they can inflict can be considerably greater.

Each type of storm, therefore, calls for an understanding of its unique threats. Napoleon may (or may not) have actually said "Luck favors the prepared," but *someone* out there had the right idea!

TORNADOES

A tornado is a violently rotating column of air extending upward from the ground to the base of a thunderstorm cloud. All of us probably have seen photographs and video of these roaring walls of dirt and debris, a tube of rising warm air that rotates rapidly. Fewer of us, thankfully, have ever been close to one.

Most intense tornadoes are spawned from supercells or rotating thunderstorms that are formed by disturbances in the upper atmosphere. A supercell is a discrete, long-lived, severe thunderstorm that forms in an environment where wind direction or speed changes sharply with height. This wind shear produces bundles of air that rotate horizontally and roll forward like a steamroller. Disturbances of this type provide the strong vertical wind shear that imparts a twisting motion to the updraft and turns a normal thunderstorm into a tornado (see illustration, opposite).

Tornadoes, with their upwardly rotating column of air, differ from storms called microbursts, which feature air blasting downward from thunderstorms. But both are localized storms and both can be very dangerous. Large hail often precedes tornadoes as a result of the intense updraft feeding into the thunderstorm.

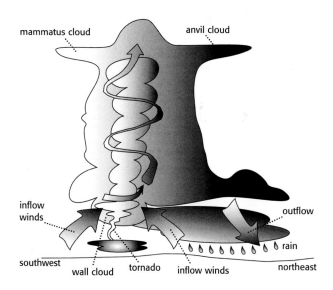

Tornadoes can develop from thunderstorms when downdrafts of cold, dry air and updrafts of warm, moist air interact with wind shear. This can cause the storm to start rotating, eventually forming a wall cloud.

While the exact process for the formation of a tornado's funnel is not known, we do know that the funnel consists of moist air that condenses into droplets. The descending funnel is made visible by these opaque, cloudlike droplets. Dust and debris on the ground begin to rotate and are sucked up into the funnel, changing the color of the tornado. Funnels can last from several seconds to more than an hour, but most only survive for about 10 minutes.

While the chance of a boatowner encountering a damaging tornado is slight, the opportunity certainly exists, particularly on the lakes and rivers of Tornado Alley, a storm-susceptible swath of the central United States. As spring-time unfolds, unstable, sun-heated air near the surface combines with strong winds aloft to start America's annual tornado activity. It normally begins in early spring in the Gulf Coast states, then the zone moves north and west toward the upper Midwest by June and July.

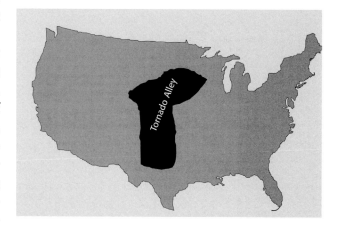

While Tornado Alley in the Great Plains states has the greatest concentration of twisters, they can occur almost anywhere in the United States.

As mentioned earlier, tornadoes can accompany hurricanes, often developing during a hurricane's journey inland, placing Atlantic Coast states at occasional risk and giving Gulf Coast states a second opportunity to get smacked.

In any given year about 1,000 tornadoes strike the United States, more than any other country. Compared to thunderstorms, whose winds can reach 100 miles per hour or more, tornadoes can produce winds of 200 miles per hour and sometimes a great deal more. The devastation from such a concentrated strike of raw energy is reason enough for boatowners to take them seriously.

Unfortunately, there is little that you can do to protect a boat from a direct hit by a tornado. With the ferocity of these winds and the almost unbelievable updraft in the funnel, almost no preventive measure can help. Damage will be extreme for a boat that is hit, but one of the strange characteristics of tornadoes is their surgical strike zone. The swath a tornado cuts on its destructive rampage can be quite narrow, often only a few hundred yards wide. Along its path, one boat may be destroyed while another, only yards away, may survive untouched. As an analogy, imagine a paved road devoid of all growth while at the curbs trees, shrubs, grass, and flowers grow undisturbed. Your boat would be destroyed if moored on the road but untouched on the grass berm.

When I lived in the Midwest, I remember seeing photographs of a tornado-damaged house that had literally been cut in half. The front was completely gone. The back half exposed the dining room with the dinner table set—dishes, glasses, and even napkins were undisturbed. Another news photograph showed a steel freight barge on the Ohio River that had been twisted like taffy, yet the American flag still fluttered in the breeze on the stern.

Your best defense during tornado season is to follow many of the hurricane preparation suggestions that appear later in this book—especially the advice for stowing loose items; practicing overkill on docking and anchor lines; and making sure your marine insurance coverage is up to date and sufficient to reimburse you for a total loss. Bring small boats into a garage or shed to protect them from flying debris and tie down larger boats on land. Even with these precautions, if you experience a direct hit, the chances of a total loss are high.

THUNDERSTORMS AND LINE SQUALLS

Another storm system of concern to boatowners is a local thunderstorm. Though thunderstorms can be found throughout the entire United States, they occur most frequently in the central and southern states. Unlucky Florida has the honor of having the highest number of thunderstorm days. Its unique geography—with warm unstable air flowing north from the Gulf of Mexico intersecting with cold air masses from the subartic, without a range of mountains to separate them—is a perfect breeding ground for thunderstorms. In Europe and Asia, the mountain ranges run east to west, convenient physical geography that disrupts thunderstorm conditions. In the

United States, the mountains run approximately north and south and do little to block these warm air–cold air collisions.

At any given moment, nearly 1,800 thunderstorms are in progress over the earth's surface. The United States gets approximately 100,000 each year and almost 1,000 of them develop into tornadoes. If only because thunderstorms are so prevalent and can be very destructive, boatowners should know more about them.

To begin, we have to understand cold fronts, which are boundaries between masses of cold and warm air, with the colder air replacing the warmer. They are identified on weather maps as solid blue lines with triangles pointing in the direction the cold air is traveling. As a cold front moves into an area, the heavier cold

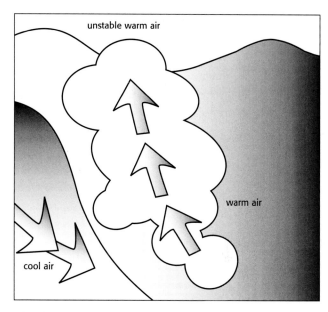

Thunderstorms are often the result of cold fronts pushing their way under warm fronts.

air pushes under the lighter warm air it is replacing. The warm air cools as it rises and, if the rising air is humid enough, the water vapor in it condenses into clouds and possibly precipitation. In the summer, an arriving cold front can trigger thunderstorms with hail, dangerous winds, and even tornadoes.

Thunderclouds can be several miles across the bottom and tower to an altitude of 40,000 feet or more. High-level winds often shred the cloud top into the familiar anvil form. Depending on the intensity and extent of the cold front, thunderstorms may occur singly, in clusters, or in lines, which is one of the reasons that several thunderstorms can affect your marina in the course of only a few hours.

All thunderstorms contain lightning. In addition to the hurricane-force winds that a thunderstorm can generate, lightning is also a real danger to boats, particularly sailboats with masts sticking up into the elements. When the buildup of positive and negative charges within a storm gets strong enough, an electrical discharge or a lightning bolt results. If this discharge is between the clouds and the ground, your boat, in a split second, is at risk of being hit by a sword of electricity of unimaginable voltage, with a temperature that approaches 50,000°F. It is therefore essential for your boat to have a well-designed lightning protection system, including proper electrical bonding and grounding to direct lightning away from people and vulnerable hardware and allow it to dissipate in the water. And you should have the entire system inspected annually by a competent marine mechanic to be sure none of the grounding connections have corroded or come loose. See the end of Chapter 8 for more on lightning protection.

Line squalls move fast and stretch from one end of the horizon to the other. (Courtesy NOAA/NWS)

Hail, from pea size up to softball size, can fall from the thunderheads and cause serious damage to boat windows and canvas. Hail takes shape several miles above the ground inside strong thunderstorms when the cloud's moisture is supercooled and freezes around nuclei like dust, salt, or frozen raindrops. Small hailstones tend to fall in large quantities near the heart of a storm, whereas larger hail gets centrifuged toward the outer edge of the storm. Though hail can cause considerable damage, it rarely kills people, although in May 1986, 100 people were killed in China from an intense hailstorm.

Then there is the threat of flash floods from the heavy rains that normally accompany thunderstorms. Flash floods should not be taken lightly, particularly by boaters who keep their craft on inland rivers and lakes—flash floods are the leading cause of death from weather-related storms.

In November 1985, thunderstorms caused a flash flood in and around Roanoke, Virginia. Torrential rain caused the Roanoke River to rise 18 feet in 6 hours, putting the downtown area under 8 feet of water. The same story could be told again and again from one part of the country to the other; boats, docks, and entire inland marinas can be swept away in minutes.

A cold front can also spawn a line squall, a fast-moving windstorm with embedded thunderstorms that develop quickly and repeatedly at its leading edge. A group of thunderstorms can form into a line squall that extends for miles and can strike quickly and with gale-force winds. They often advertise themselves with a rolling, black wall that starts at the horizon and seems to be tumbling over everything before it. The sharper, darker, and lower the front edge of the line squall looks, the more powerful it will be.

The best protection against being caught by surprise by a thunderstorm or line squall is to listen to (or read online) the marine weather forecast at least hourly if there is the slightest suspicion of severe weather. But because these storms cover relatively small areas and are short lived, it is difficult—and often impossible—to track their development. It takes a trained radar operator looking at the structure of a thunderstorm to be able to give even a few minutes' warning. The best way to protect your boat is to ensure that it is always tied up properly, with plenty of strong lines secured to sound foundations.

NOR'EASTERS

A nor'easter (or northeaster, if you prefer) is a circular storm that forms off the northeastern coast of the United States. With humid air and gale-force winds, nor'easters bring heavy, cold rains in the summer months and blizzards in the winter. These storms are not to be trifled with: a nor'easter on Ash Wednesday, 1962, caused extensive destruction from North Carolina to New York, and an October 1991 nor'easter off the Massachusetts coast became positively famous in a bestselling nonfiction book and a major Hollywood production called *The Perfect Storm*. Though their winds are generally below hurricane force, nor'easters can last from several days to a week or more, giving the wind time to generate large waves and significant storm surge.

KEEP A WEATHER EYE OUT

Paying attention to developing storms is something you have to learn, sometimes the hard way.

As a teenager, I was caught in a summer thunderstorm while sailing a Lightning on the Mississippi River, just north of St. Louis, Missouri. A buddy and I were out for an afternoon sail. Two brown paper bags with lunchtime sandwiches were stowed in the locker. A warm, upriver breeze scooted us along against the current, and all was well until Jake, shielding his eyes from the sun, said, "What's that?" I looked over the trees to the west and saw a black wall of clouds tumbling toward us only seconds before the wind and rain hit. The little Lightning and our inexperience were no match for the tumult that tore at us. Before we could drop sails or even turn into the wind, we were on our side, sails in the water, and being pushed toward the rocky shore. Moments later we ground onto the beach, tied the boat to a tree, and crawled soaking-wet into a limestone cave. Wet, cold, and as frightened as Tom Sawyer in his cave, we had to spend that night and the next morning there before the Coast Guard found us. We had been hit by an afternoon line squall, one of the fastest-moving weather phenomena a boater can experience.

In a sense, we were fortunate to be out on open water. But neglected boats at anchor with worn lines or in their slips with inadequate fenders may not fare as well. A summer line squall may only last a few minutes but can do as much damage to an unprepared boat as a hurricane.

Like northern hemisphere hurricanes, nor'easters circulate counterclockwise. In New England, this means that the winds come off the ocean toward the shore from an easterly or northeasterly direction while the storm's center is still far to the south. The winds often travel great distances across the ocean before reaching the shore, and this long fetch produces huge waves and even influences the height of tides. Flood tides may be pushed far higher than normal, and the constant offshore breeze, lasting several days, along with tide changes may prevent tides from ebbing out to sea, causing rivers to back up and creating widespread inland flooding.

Mike Keyworth has been the manager of Brewer Cove Haven Marina in Barrington, Rhode Island, for 20 years, and he has seen his share of nor'easters and hurricanes. He says that boatowners should prepare for a nor'easter as they would for a hurricane. Because the Northeast has big tide ranges, which require marinas to have floating docks with at least 14-foot pilings, docked boats are in a pretty good position to cope with the storm surge from either type of storm.

The physical location and orientation of a marina relative to storm winds and storm surge is one of the most significant factors for a boatowner to consider when choosing a berth for a boat in the Northeast or, for that matter, almost anywhere else in the country. One facility might be destroyed by a nor'easter, while a neighboring marina may come through almost unscathed due to better natural protection from the storm's path. The next storm could well reverse the situation. However, marinas that are protected from open water and have well-engineered and well-maintained docks in addition to a well-thought-out and well-executed hurricane plan will generally come through the tumult with little damage.

REGIONAL WINDS

Among the least well known yet most interesting weather phenomena are regional winds not associated with storms. These local events are found in most parts of the world, and, at last count, there were 240 named winds worldwide. North America has many, including the Taku in Alaska, the Santa Ana in California, the Sundowner on the Southern California coast, the Diablo in northern California, the Chinook in the Rocky Mountains, and the Norther in the southern plains.

The Santa Ana winds, for example, occur in southwest California when cold, high-pressure air in the Great Basin spills through mountain passes to the west and descends toward the coast. As the air sinks, it heats *adiabatically* (as a result of increasing air pressure). This hot, dry air mass can hit Southern California with sustained northeasterly winds well over 25 miles per hour and gusts up to 100, creating a hazard to boats in the Los Angeles basin and San Diego County. Santa Anas occur from October through March, with autumn being the prime season.

Similar to the Santa Ana is the Tehuantepecer, violent winds that cause occasional devastation to commercial ships and pleasure boats alike in the Gulf of Tehuantepec, south of southwestern Mexico and adjacent to Guatemala. These winds originate as cold winds in the Gulf of Mexico, then they cross the isthmus, funneling through mountain passes, and become warm and dry as they descend. By the time they reach the coast, wind speeds may be over 100 miles per hour, and the winds may extend up to 100 miles out to sea.

Quite different but also potentially disastrous is the katabatic Taku wind of Alaska. Katabatic winds are created when an area of high-pressure, cold air—like that over a mountain glacier—displaces warmer, less-dense air at the side of a mountain. The cold air flows below the warm air and down the slope with incredible speed. (Anabatic winds are the opposite—winds that flow up slopes.) Migael Scherer, author of *A Cruising Guide to Puget Sound and the San Juan Islands*, has been through them. She and her husband lived aboard a 50-foot, heavy-displacement ketch in Juneau, Alaska, a city at the foot of the 3,000-foot-high coastal mountain range that is topped with a glacier. Though this is not your typical cruising ground, the spectacular beauty of fir-covered islands nestled beneath snow capped mountains makes it one of the country's last cruising frontiers.

The Taku wind begins as cold air hurtles down the steep slope of the glacier. Accelerating up to 100 miles per hour, it slams into Juneau harbor without warning. But, as Migael and her husband learned, boatowners expect these katabatic winds, so before winter begins, they prepare. Newcomers listen to the advice that is passed around, as conditions in Juneau are different from almost anywhere else. Migael recounts that their preparations include the following:

All running rigging is removed. All halyards but one are removed to reduce windage and prevent the noise of slapping halyards. Sails are bagged and stowed. Roller furling gear is taken down and stowed below. Lines are doubled and chafing gear religiously applied. Long spring lines are set, as tides in the area normally run 10 to 12 feet, with up to 20-foot tides during a high-high and low-low. Fuel is topped off and fenders are put out.

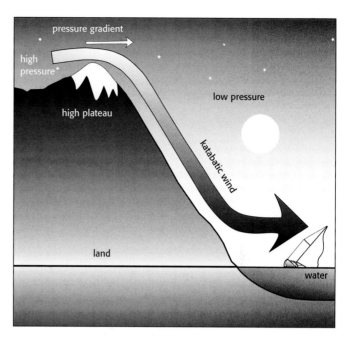

When an area of high pressure forces a mass of cold air to the edge of a mountain or plateau, the cold air tumbles down the slope as a katabatic wind.

But, most importantly, the whole boat is covered with a structure of PVC pipe and polyethylene sheeting that is tied to the boat with bungee cords. The stretchable cords let the structure move and give, where a more rigid construction might blow away. The cover helps keep the boat warm, and snow or ice can be easily knocked off. Without the plastic cover, snow and ice could pile up with enough weight to sink some boats.

These precautions won't guarantee Juneau boaters immunity from the Taku, but at least they've done what they can.

THREAT SUMMARY

Wind

Winds of 50 to 75 miles per hour in thunderstorms and nor'easters, 100+ miles per hour in hurricanes, and 200+ miles per hour in tornadoes are realistic. Just put your arm out of the car window at 60 miles per hour to see what a violent, quick-striking thunderstorm feels like, then imagine it doubled or tripled—and how such a wind could affect the various items on your boat. This should be enough incentive to move vulnerable equipment and store it in a safe place.

Flying debris can be a serious threat to you and your boat. Once you have secured your boat and all its accessories, talk to your neighbors. If necessary, help them get their boats in shape to withstand the coming storm. Help them tie down everything they can't remove. In the long run, your efforts will help you both.

Storm Surge

Storm surge—the onshore rush of sea or lake water caused by high winds—can be very dangerous. The low pressure and high winds of the storm can combine to raise the water level from a few feet in a minor storm to 15 to 20 feet in a major hurricane. The height of the surge within the eye of a hurricane can be almost double compared to the surge outside the eye, due to the extreme low pressure in the eye pulling the sea surface upward.

Keep in mind that marinas and mooring fields in protected bays may actually encounter higher surges than coastal areas because high winds can pile up water in the bay and keep it trapped there.

Tides

The timing of a storm's landfall relative to the state of the tide can be critical. If a storm hits at high tide, the probability of severe damage increases because any storm surge will be lifted that much higher. On the other hand, if a storm hits at low tide, damage should be lower.

Spring tides are especially strong tides (higher high tides and lower low tides) that occur when the earth, sun, and moon are almost aligned. (Spring tides have nothing to do with the spring season.) This alignment occurs at every full moon and new moon. If storm surge hits at a spring high tide, it will be that much higher again, and if it hits at a spring low tide, then consider yourself lucky.

The proxigean spring tide is a rare, unusually high tide that occurs when the moon is both unusually close to the earth (at its closest perigee, called the proxigee) and in the new moon phase (when the moon is between the sun and the earth). The proxigean spring tide occurs at most once every 1.5 years.

Neap tides are especially weak tides. They occur when the gravitational forces of the moon and the sun are perpendicular to one another (with respect to the earth). Neap tides occur during quarter moons.

Rain

The amount of rain that can fall in a thunderstorm or hurricane can be significant, leading to flooding, swift currents, and even swamped boats. For example, 21 inches of rain fell in a 24-hour period on Americus, Georgia, from Tropical Storm Alberto in July 1994, and 43—yes, 43—inches of rain fell in a 24-hour period on Alvin, Texas, from Tropical Storm Claudette in July 1979. It makes sense that a slow-moving storm will deposit enormous quantities of rain whereas a fast-moving storm will sweep through an area quickly and dump less rain. So keep in mind that more rain damage will occur from a storm that lingers for a long time and continues to dump rain on your boat and home.

Inland Flooding

It has been estimated that more than half of all deaths from tropical storms came from freshwater flooding. This is a surprising statistic for some of us. News reports often focus on coastal destruction. We don't often consider the enormous damage caused by inland flooding when a hurricane moves to its death in the interior. Even after seeing on TV all the damage done by the four 2004 hurricanes in Florida, it is an eye-opener to discover that a large percentage of the damage caused by those storms came from inland flooding and tornadoes. Hurricane Katrina's enormous damage to the city of New Orleans came from the levees breaking, which allowed Lake Pontchartrain to flood the city.

4 Marine Insurance

The love/hate relationship many boatowners have with marine insurance is not unwarranted. Most of us appreciate the peace of mind that it confers throughout the year, and we especially appreciate it when we have a claim—if action on the claim is prompt and we perceive the settlement as fair. On the other hand, many of us are also confused by the entire insurance process: we don't know what kind of coverage we need or don't need; we may resent the premiums associated with the level of coverage that our lender demands; and we can become extremely dissatisfied when action on a claim is slow or we perceive the settlement as unfair. Ambivalent as we may be, most of us—particularly those who live in areas often hit by severe storms—are concerned about the potential for loss and acknowledge the necessity for good insurance coverage. Thus, the only real question is, what *is* good insurance coverage?

INSURANCE POLICIES

As a general rule, if you don't understand the terminology of your policy, ask your agent. If he or she doesn't make it clear to you, call a company representative who can give you accurate advice. Explain your specific concerns to the representative, and tell him or her where and how you will operate your boat.

Even for smaller boats, it is advisable to take out a separate marine policy, not add it to your homeowner's policy. A marine policy includes many conditions not addressed in a typical homeowner's policy. It is usually written on an all-risk basis, covering both physical damage and owner's liability. Most marine policies also offer important optional coverage such as passenger liability, equipment, trailers, and waterskiing liability. Limits and deductibles vary with each company's programs.

Most policies offer hull and equipment coverage for either agreed value or actual cash value. If agreed value applies, the boatowner will be paid for whatever value the insurer and boatowner *agreed to* in the case of a total loss. Under an actual cash value policy, the boatowner will receive the *insured* value of the boat or the actual cash value (depreciated value), whichever is less. Therefore, with an agreed-to policy, the boatowner can stipulate (and pay for) the replacement value of the boat; replacement cost coverage on partial losses generally includes everything except sails, canvas, batteries, outboard engines, and machinery. And even these can be insured by some policies. With an insured-value policy, the owner is covered only up to the depreciated value of the boat.

Under protection and indemnity liability, the policy should cover bodily injury, property damage, and wreck removal. Your agent should be able to advise you on how much coverage is reasonable for each of these forms of liability.

The policy should also cover medical payments for the insured and guests, uninsured bodily injury coverage for the insured, personal property coverage for personal effects or sporting gear, and last but not least, towing. While many of these forms of coverage aren't directly related to storm damage, most may be at least incidental to it, and all of them are highly advisable from a more general view of insurance coverage in any case.

Other forms of coverage to consider include salvage charges (see Chapter 12), legal defense costs, pollution and contamination containment, removal expenses, and boat trailer loss.

Some policies have a special deductible for damage from named hurricanes and/or tropical storms, which helps reduce the cost to the insurance company from huge claims that result from hurricanes. If you live in a hurricane-prone area of the country, be especially aware of this clause since it applies to the situation where damage to your boat is most likely.

Almost all policies define geographical limits of navigation under which the boat is insured. If you take your boat outside these defined geographical limits, you must purchase an addendum to temporarily expand the policy's coverage. If you go outside the limits of navigation without the insurance addendum, you may be "naked"— have no coverage at all.

Your policy may also place limits on the distance you can trailer your boat, and it may specify different coverage if your boat is moved by a trucking company.

The premium is usually based on the size of the boat, its horsepower, the range of navigation, and operator experience. Most insurers require surveys for boats and yachts more than 10 years old. Boats older than 25 years are generally written under special "seasoned yacht" boat programs. Some carriers require a surcharge of up to 30 percent for navigation in Florida and the Gulf Coast because of the frequency of hurricanes and catastrophic losses in this area.

Unfortunately, insurance premiums and deductibles have gone up dramatically due to heavy claims after the 2004 and 2005 hurricane seasons. In Florida, absentee boatowners are even being turned down by many insurance companies. Their assumption is that absentee owners will not make adequate prestorm preparations. You may be able to overcome this objection if you can show the insurer a written hurricane plan that identifies another knowledgeable person (such as a management company or a delivery captain) who will be on standby to implement a storm-preparation plan (see the sidebar, opposite).

Most insurers offer discounts for various factors that reduce the level of risk. These include owner's attendance of a boating safety course, Coast Guard safety inspections, and installation of theft detection devices and alarm systems.

Here are some questions to ask your agent before purchasing yacht insurance:

- Is hull and equipment coverage based on an agreed value?
- Are replacement costs used on partial losses?
- Is wreck removal included in the liability coverage?
- Are gelcoat and paint depreciated?
- Does the policy carry a "named storm" deductible (see below)?
- Is the dinghy included?
- Are sails, outboard, and accessories depreciated at the time of loss?
- What limit is there on land transportation?
- Is there any pollution coverage?
- What is the navigational warranty?

Marine insurance policies, even more so than other insurance coverage, are full of arcane definitions that date back to early British law. Much is guided by the term "act of God," which usually means that if a storm destroys your boat, you are not held responsible as long as "negligent behavior" was not behind the damage. Therefore, negligent behavior—such as a powerboat in a slip with a nonworking engine, or a leaky sailboat already half-filled with water before a storm—is an exclusion from an act of God.

"Reasonable and prudent" defines the boatowner's responsibility to protect the boat from any further damages, prevent the boat from damaging others, and shield it from potential looting, regardless of its condition. Virtually every marine insurance policy contains this provision. In essence, your insurance policy obligates you to take all reasonable actions to preserve the boat from further loss and damage to itself and to other boats.

"Latent defect" is a term that covers a defect in the boat that is not detected in a normal inspection. Most often, a latent defect relates to a manufacturing defect, not a loss caused by a storm as an act of God. Therefore, it is almost impossible to use a latent defect as the basis of a claim for storm-related damage.

There will be a policy deductible for damage caused by a named storm or named windstorm, which refers to hurricanes and all other tropical weather patterns that are given specific names or numbers (e.g., Hurricane Andrew, Tropical Storm Mitch, Tropical Depression Number Seven). It generally applies from the time the named storm impacts an area until 72 hours after the storm departs. The geographical area of coverage affected by a named windstorm clause is often defined as an area encompassed by a circle whose radius does not exceed 150 nautical miles from the path of the storm's forward travel.

Some companies refer to "removal from grounding" as towing. However, towing could actually damage a grounded vessel if not done correctly. Other companies interpret a hard grounding as salvage. We will look at salvage in detail in Chapter 12.

Some policies pay all the costs of wreck removal. Others don't cover it at all. Some may pay off a total loss claim on the boat but leave the owner responsible for the boat's removal. If a wreck breaks up and its debris causes damage to another boat, liability can be severe.

These and other problem areas show the difficulty of choosing a marine insurance policy. Too often, a boatowner has no idea what is covered until a problem has occurred, when it is too late to make a change in the policy. Shop around and read policies carefully. Determine which of the above-named clauses and conditions should be negotiated with your insurance agent, and then add those coverages to your policy.

> ### AN OPTION FOR ABSENTEE OWNERS
>
> Absentee boatowners—owners who live in one place and keep their boat elsewhere—may be subject to (legal) discrimination by insurance companies, partly on the rationale that they are not able to make timely storm preparations. Some marinas offer storm-prep services that not only protect your boat but make it more insurable as well.
>
> River Forest Yachting Center (www.riverforestyc.com), near Stuart, Florida, for example, has one indoor storage facility rated for winds up to 145 miles per hour where boats up to 65 feet long are stored; another indoor facility for smaller craft; and an outdoor storage area, equipped with tie-down points set in cement pads, for boats on jack stands. In the event of a storm warning, River Forest will store an owner's boat as agreed upon under the terms of the marina's Hurricane Club agreement, which it says can save an absentee owner up to 20 percent on his or her insurance.

INSURANCE CLAIMS

If your boat has been damaged, contact your insurance agent as soon as possible and ask for instructions on what to do until your adjuster arrives. Use your up-to-date inventory to assess those items that have been damaged and have them included in a summary for the adjuster. Photograph the damaged items.

Don't make any permanent repairs, except those necessary to prevent further damage, until your insurance company has inspected the boat, and you have reached an agreement on the cost of repairs. Many insurance companies have a legal right to inspect your boat in its damaged condition and may refuse to pay you for any damage repaired before it has been inspected. Keep all receipts from immediately necessary repairs to include with your photographs and damage report. If the expenses you submit to your insurance company for securing the boat from further damage and providing security are reasonable, your policy will probably cover any money spent prior to having an adjuster inspect the boat.

Looting is a possibility when a boat has been washed into a public area. The police will probably be busy with more serious storm-related problems and not have the time or manpower to watch over your stranded boat. The cost of hiring security to watch over the boat may also be covered by your policy as a justifiable expense.

Insurance adjusters are usually assigned by the insurance company to visit your boat to report on the damage and estimate the costs of repair, which they forward to the insurance company for action. Many of these adjusters are independent appraisers who are contract-hired by the insurance company. They are not there to cheat you out of a fair settlement but to make an honest appraisal of the cost of repair.

If possible, be present to work with the adjuster, pointing out the various problem areas, some of which may not be obvious to someone unfamiliar with your boat. Your help in pointing out storm-related problems will be appreciated. A cordial, respectful conversation with the adjuster will help your cause. Volunteering too much irrelevant or potentially damaging information or getting irritated with the adjuster will not. Adjusters who are working an area after a storm are often heavily stressed, and work very long hours to get to all the people with registered claims as quickly as possible. They are, after all, only human and will appreciate your help and a show of respect.

Your Duties

Most insurance companies and the policies they write require you to abide by all of the following in the event of a loss:

- Immediately take all possible steps to minimize the loss and protect the vessel from further loss. (You are not, however, obligated to put yourself at personal risk.) Failure to do so may invalidate your insurance coverage or reduce the amount of any claim.
- As soon as possible, notify your insurance company of the loss and its circumstances.
- Comply with any reasonable request made of you by your insurance company with regard to the loss.
- Advise the police, Coast Guard, or any appropriate authority of the loss and its circumstances.
- Give your insurance company an opportunity to examine the damaged property before it is repaired or discarded.
- Submit a claim form and/or a statement describing the loss, together with two estimates of repair costs and/or records to substantiate the amount of the loss.
- Neither assume obligation nor admit liability to any other party without your insurance company's written permission to do so.

- Immediately forward to your insurance company any legal papers or notices received in connection with the loss.

- Cooperate with your insurance company in the investigation, defense, or settlement of any loss, and agree to be examined under oath if they so request.

- Assist your insurance company in obtaining copies of medical records and reports.

- Give a notarized statement if the company requests one.

- Give your insurance company proof of loss and discharge of liability once you have agreed to the amount of the claim under the insurance agreement.

- Preserve any right of recovery from others. When your insurance company pays a loss, you have basically signed over your right to further remuneration, and your right to recover becomes theirs. If you recover money from any other source, it belongs to your insurance company, up to the amount of their payment to you plus legal fees and expenses. You must also cooperate with the company to recover the losses they pay.

MARITIME LIENS

Boats are subject to special liens (legal claims) called maritime liens. Maritime law considers that a lien is in place as soon as money is owed, and paperwork is not even necessary! Every technician, marina, or repair shop that does repair work on your boat can be considered to have a lien against him/it until the bill is paid.

Those of us who pay our repair bills as requested usually do not need to be concerned by this, but under a storm situation, unusual conditions may arise involving salvage, towing, legal defense, and extremely large repair bills. If your insurance policy covers salvage, towing, legal defense, and replacement costs, you should experience little financial burden in the event of a dispute with the service provider. Whenever possible, protect your interests by having all work carefully defined in writing before it commences, and upon completion, document that the work was performed as requested.

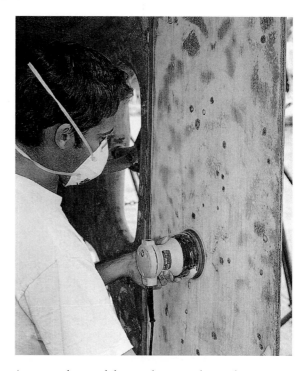

Anytime a boatyard does work on your boat, a lien is in place until the bill is paid. Find out ahead of time what your insurance will cover. (David Westphal photo, courtesy *The Hinckley Guide to Yacht Care*)

5 Creating a Plan

It has been demonstrated over and over that boats whose owners have a well-rehearsed storm-preparation plan stand a far better chance of surviving a severe storm than those who make panic-stricken preparations at the last minute. All boatowners should develop a plan well before hurricane season. Depending on what kind of boat you own, where you keep it, and where you live, your plan may be complex, or as simple as putting the boat on a trailer and taking it home to your garage. No two boatowners will have exactly the same strategy.

In developing your plan, evaluate every contingency and include everything you can think of to protect your boat (you should have a plan to protect your home and family too). Write down your plan to prevent confusion and avoid forgetting anything. When a hurricane approaches, an enormous amount of work must be done in a short period of time. Since everyone else will be busy with their own last-minute preparations, getting help from friends and neighbors will be problematic unless firm commitments are already in place.

Be prepared for the possibility that you may be away when a storm is due and not able to get to your boat in time to put your plan into action. Make sure another member of your family is fully aware of the plan and capable of implementing it if you cannot return in time. Or designate someone else who can take over in your absence. In either case, let your marina know the name and contact information of the person(s) who will be responsible for storm preparations. (You place undue hardship on marina personnel if you don't inform them of your storm plan ahead of time and when you put it into effect.) Make sure your designated helper's own personal responsibilities and capabilities allow him or her to pitch in effectively before the storm.

Your plan should include detailed instructions to remind you what must be done to prepare your boat to ride out a storm and the necessary actions to comply with your marina's emergency plan, if applicable. Take into consideration neighboring boatowners, whose preparations (or lack thereof) may affect yours. Keep in mind that marina personnel will probably not have the time or staff to assist you prior to a storm's approach; they will be busy implementing the marina's storm preparedness plan and dealing with any emergency situations that develop.

Note: In addition to your storm-prep plan for your boat, you must also have a plan for protecting your home and loved ones; they should take priority over the boat. Those plans are beyond the scope of this book, but make those preparations before preparing your boat.

To avoid a last-minute mad scramble to the chandlery or hardware store, and the likelihood that necessary supplies will be sold out, get everything you need for storm preparation well before storm warnings are issued—in other words, before hurricane season begins. Be sure you have gathered all the necessary gear and supplies into readily available kits to avoid a frantic, futile, frustrating "Honey, where is the . . . ?" shouting match.

The list below identifies some materials you might want to stock up on before hurricane season. Some you will use for preparations immediately before a storm, while others are for a longer-term approach to storm preparation and meant to last a full season or more. No single storm situation will make use of all of them; see the following chapters for details on their use.

WORK WITH YOUR MARINA'S MANAGEMENT

Mike Keyworth, manager of Brewer Cove Haven Marina in Barrington, Rhode Island (www.byy.com/barrington), has found that boatowners generally follow the path of least resistance and will wait until the last minute to make storm preparations. For this reason, he makes a concerted effort to apprise each owner of the seriousness of each approaching storm and urges them to make early preparations.

The marina's land storage area is 12 feet above mean high water, so it is able to offer early haulout for those boatowners who wish it. Boatowners at marinas that have low-lying land storage areas may not be as eager to store their craft on land.

Mike has four suggestions for his clients:

1. Check, and if necessary revise, your marine insurance policy. Look carefully at the policy provisions, particularly the full-loss conditions.
2. Make preparations early; when the storm gets close to landfall there will likely be much confusion, and Murphy's Law (anything that can go wrong will go wrong) will inevitably kick in.
3. Provide the marina with a copy of your personal storm plan, including all relevant personal contact and boat information.
4. Last and most important: *Do not stay on your boat during the storm!*

Mike sums up by saying, "Do the best you can to prepare the boat for the storm and then go home and wait." See Appendix D for Brewer Cove Haven Marina's storm preparation policies.

KEY STORM PREPARATION SUPPLIES

storm anchor(s) with associated ground tackle
additional heavy anchor rode
extra chain
oversized shackles
heavier, longer docking lines
larger cleats for your boat and the dock
chafing gear
extra heavy-duty fenders
tie-down straps

duct tape
polyethylene sheeting
tarps
general-duty rope
garbage bags
rags
extra batteries for your radio
cleaning supplies
underwater-setting epoxy putty (e.g., Marine-Tex)
tapered plugs for through-hulls

TIMING

As a storm approaches, begin implementing your plan's early stages, monitoring the media to know the storm's predicted time and place of landfall, direction of approach, and wind strength (see Chapter 6). From that information, determine the most likely direction of winds you will face (remember that this will depend on which side of the eye passes your location). Estimate the height of the anticipated storm surge, and look at the tide tables to determine if it will come on top of a high or low tide. From this information, decide whether to leave the boat where it is or move it. If you decide to leave it where it is, then decide whether to leave it in the water or store it on land. Then call your helpers/friends and implement your plan.

Storm preparations for your boat should be completed 48 hours in advance of a hurricane's projected arrival. Waiting until the last minute might prevent you from getting to the boat due to road closures and other storm-related problems. If your plan involves moving the boat to a safer location, do not wait until weather conditions have deteriorated, bridges are locked down, traffic from other boats is heavy, and darkness falls. Any of these problems may rob you of success.

If you live in an area with drawbridges, keep in mind that the Department of Transportation officials who operate the drawbridges often have no choice about the timing of closures. Evacuation orders from the state's governor or county emergency preparedness officials may require them to keep the bridge lowered (i.e., closed to boat traffic) when moving people out of high-risk areas becomes the top priority. The last thing officials want is to have a mass evacuation held up because a bridge is open for a passing boat. Their worst fear is that a swing bridge will be damaged and become inoperable. This happened in September 1989 during Hurricane Hugo in Charleston, South Carolina, to the Ben Sawyer Bridge, which connected two islands to the mainland. The hurricane dislodged the abutments, rotated the swing bridge, and tipped the superstructure so that one end fell into the river.

Therefore as a boatowner, pay strict attention to alerts from the Coast Guard regarding potential bridge closings when a hurricane threatens. Getting caught by a closed bridge can cause panic, and possibly a disaster if you are forced to dramatically switch plans, literally in midstream. How about having a plan B as well as a plan A?

Use the following list as the basis for developing a personalized plan specific to your boat and situation. Revise the order of items as you feel appropriate. Assign time flags to ensure that each action will be done in proper order and that nothing will be missed in the hectic hours before a storm.

STORM PREPARATION CHECKLIST

Preseason Tasks

1. Develop a plan early—well before the storm season begins. Prepare a checklist of what you must do to secure your boat.
2. Scout out alternative storage locations for your boat and develop a second plan; the first will have the boat remain at its regular location, and the other will deal with moving it to another location (see Chapter 7).
3. Assign an alternate contact person to stand in for you if you cannot get to the boat on time.
4. Make any physical improvements that will contribute to your boat's safety. These could include repairs or upgrades to gear and hardware on your boat and on your mooring (see Chapter 9), slip, or dock (see Chapter 8).
5. Review your boat insurance and update it as necessary (see Chapter 4).
6. Talk to neighboring boatowners to coordinate storm preparations.
7. Obtain the gear and supplies you will need to prepare your boat for the storm, and to clean up afterward. Pack them into readily accessible kits, and put them in a secure place. (See the list of storm supplies on pages 39–40.)
8. Take an inventory of all items on the boat and identify those you will remove and those you will leave on board. Photographic or video documentation can sometimes help capture items you miss in a written inventory, and may be a great help in making an insurance claim.
9. Identify all important records such as your lease agreement with the marina, your insurance policies, your boat equipment inventory, and boat identification documents. If any of these are kept on the boat, they should be on your list of items to remove prior to a storm.
10. Contact your marina or yacht club for their mandatory storm preparedness requirements. Know your responsibilities and understand your potential liabilities (see below).
11. Inform your marina how you will implement your plan (that they already have a copy of): they need to know whether you will stay put, run for shelter, or be hauled for land storage.
12. Practice your plan. Are supplies like tarps, extra lines, and tool kits readily available and in a safe place? If you are planning to move the boat to a

safer location, choose a sunny day and make a trial run. Note maximum travel time, bridge-opening schedule (if applicable), bottom type, and anchor tackle needed. When setting a departure time in the plan, allow plenty of extra time as bridge openings and boat traffic will probably not be normal prior to a storm.

13. Keep your laptop battery fully charged.

Hurricane Warning Is Announced (or Within 48 to 60 Hours of Predicted Landfall)

1. Make the decision to move or stay put.
2. Advise your alternate contact if you cannot go to the boat.
3. Check your list of equipment to take to the boat. Your checklist should include tarps, extra lines, tool kits, extra chafing gear, duct tape, appropriately sized tapered softwood plugs for each through-hull, and bailing buckets.
4. Update boat inventory to include any changes since the list was compiled.
5. Put fresh batteries in your portable radio.
6. Remove easily damaged and/or important interior items, such as cushions, clothing, bedding, charts, logbook, radio license, insurance papers, and boat registration.
7. Remove and store all vulnerable installations, such as antennas, wind generators, outriggers, biminis, enclosures, tower tops, lightweight deck anchors, flagpoles, folding swim ladders, life rafts, and spinnaker poles (see Chapter 10).
8. If possible, remove all electronic equipment, including radar, GPS, VHF radios, and depth finders.
9. Remove and store all loose items on deck, such as chairs, canvas, life rings, boat hooks, fender boards, dinghies, grills, propane tanks, spare fuel tanks, outboard motors latched to the stern rail, and fans (see Chapter 10).
10. Remove valuables from the boat.
11. Charge the boat's house batteries so they will have a full charge.
12. Clean the bilge so debris will not clog the pumps.
13. Clean the bilge pump strainers.
14. Close all through-hull connections and plug the exhaust port.
15. Tape over the fuel and water tank vents on the side of the hull.
16. Tape over the instruments, switches, and electrical panel.
17. Stuff a rag into the anchor hawsepipe.
18. Check that cockpit drains are clear.
19. Remove or lash the boom to stern cleats and tighten down the vang.

20. Tie off the halyards.
21. At a slip (see Chapter 8):

- Tie up in the center of the slip with your bow facing the expected direction of the wind.
- Double all lines and add chafing gear.
- Make docking lines taut at mid-tide mark on pilings. Remember, eye-spliced ends go on the boat, not on a dock cleat.

22. At mooring:

- Double the mooring pendant.
- Check tackle for wear.
- Let out additional scope to at least 10:1 (see Chapter 9).

23. At anchor:

- Use storm tackle and place anchors at predetermined locations (see Chapter 9)

24. Tape all dorades, vents, hatches, windows, and the companionway entrance.
25. Keep abreast of storm progress through websites, TV, and radio (see Chapter 6).
26. Inform insurance agent if any relevant changes have been made since your preseason review of the policy.
27. Secure the dock box.
28. If you have a dinghy in the boatyard, move it home or to a more secure location.
29. Help neighboring boatowners.

Hurricane Watch Is Announced (or Within 24 to 48 Hours of Landfall)

1. Check again that all seacocks are closed and label them. Put a note by the control panel to remind you they are closed.
2. Check that engine fuel valves are closed at the tank.
3. Check that the propane valve is shut off at the tank (if the tank hasn't been removed).
4. Check storm lines and chafing gear. Apply additional chafing gear as needed (see Chapter 8).
5. Leave extra dock lines in the cockpit for marina staff to use if needed.
6. Be sure the dock is clear of lines so emergency personnel can get to the boats.
7. Check that fenders are in place on open-water side of boat for protection from other boats (see Chapter 8).

8. Once procedures are complete, photograph or videotape the boat inside and out for insurance purposes.
9. Remove and store dock steps.
10. Help neighboring boatowners.
11. Advise marina or yacht club staff that the boat is secure and where to reach you.

During the Storm

1. Do not stay on the boat during the storm under any circumstances. Go home and protect your house and family.
2. Monitor the situation on the radio or via other media.

After the Storm

1. Monitor your local radio stations, as they will broadcast updated weather information, bridge reopenings, and the official clearance for reentering evacuated areas.
2. Bring your cleaning kit to the boat, including garbage bags for trash and debris removal from the cockpit and the bilge.
3. If the boat is damaged, be very careful when boarding it.
4. Photograph or videotape any damage to the boat or its contents.
5. Remove all traces of debris, mud, salt, and rainwater. Apply anticorrosion spray to protect metal surfaces exposed to salt.
6. If there has been damage to the boat, secure it from further damage, then call your insurance agent.
7. Open all the hatches, ports, and companionways to get fresh, drying air belowdeck.
8. Use duct tape to temporarily seal damaged hatches or areas that have leaked.
9. If you didn't remove the cushions, bedding, and clothing before the storm, take any that are wet and put them out to dry.
10. Check the dock or anchor lines for chafe. Repair or replace as needed.
11. Check your electric panel connections to be sure they are dry and safe.
12. Use your checklist to reinstall equipment and refit the boat.
13. If your boat sank, the engine should be pickled as soon as possible after the boat is raised (see Chapter 11).
14. Use fresh water to flush any saltwater-soaked items that may corrode.
15. If the boat ended up in a public place, call your insurance agent to discuss hiring a security guard to watch over the boat. This expense may be covered under your policy.
16. Help neighboring boatowners.

For more on what to do after a hurricane, see Chapter 11, Recovering and Restoring Your Boat.

A MARINA LEARNS ITS LESSONS

Between 1954 and 2000, fourteen major hurricanes made landfall in the area of Wrightsville Beach, North Carolina, with wind speeds ranging from 65 to 125 miles per hour. Located just off the Intracoastal Waterway, Seapath Yacht Club (www .seapathmarina.com), a "boataminium" marina, endured all of them.

The worst damage was in 1996, when Hurricane Fran made landfall on September 5 as a Category 3 storm with winds over 100 miles per hour. Fran was the most damaging hurricane to hit the area in more than 40 years, with much of the destruction caused by storm surge. Four feet of water swept through Seapath's dock house at the end of the pier. Most of the docks floated free of their pilings, and while a few of them came back down in approximately the right place, most were left hanging. Overall, the docks were a total loss, and the facility needed a complete renovation. Marjorie Megiverin, who wrote about the history of Seapath in her book *Pathway to the Sea*, tells how the club rebuilt after the storm:

The first task was to remove debris and make the property safe for the boatowners and contractors. The remnants of "A" dock, the fuel dock, and the dock house were hauled away, and the remaining docks were patched up so they could be used temporarily.

Then came the arduous process of assessing the damage and planning the rebuilding. The result was a 2-inch-thick manual of drawings and specifications that not only served as the guide for the reconstruction but documented the insurance claim as well.

Hurricane Fran taught valuable lessons. The Seapath staff learned that pilings had to be taller to allow flotation docks to float 6 feet higher than before. They also learned that the finger piers needed to extend all the way out to the tie-off pilings, not end several feet short of them. These improvements would logically strengthen the entire dock system by tying all the components together more tightly.

The plan called for all docks to be replaced, the fuel delivery equipment upgraded, and the dock house rehabilitated and surrounded by higher retaining walls. Significant upgrades elsewhere also greatly improved the facility. An assessment was levied on the Club's clients that added additional money to the insurance adjustment.

After the main "A" dock was replaced, the rebuilding of the other docks presented a logistical problem. The client docks were 95 percent filled with boats; where could these boats go while the new docks were being built? The solution called for a synchronized water ballet.

The new docks were built in 32-foot sections in the parking lot. After flotation was attached, the docks were lifted by crane and placed in the water. One by one, they were towed into the large basin between "A" and "B" docks that served as the staging area. Here, dock boxes and power pedestals, electric and telephone cables, water lines, and cable TV lines were installed, then the sections were joined together into new 500-foot-long docks. Boats were tied off to the pilings, and the old docks were towed away for demolition. Each new dock was then towed into place and the clients' boats returned to their berths.

Repairs were completed in 15 months with virtually no disruption to the boat-owners. When the job was finished, the yacht club commodore and commanders agreed that the marina should be upgraded every 20 years to employ the latest in technology and prevent equipment failures. A reserve fund was created to enable this to occur.

Three years later, Hurricane Floyd hit as a Category 2 storm on September 16, 1999, at the mouth of the Cape Fear River only a few miles from Seapath Yacht Club. Peak winds gusted to 120 miles per hour and 19 inches of rain fell. Yet the damage to the club cost a mere $15,000. The surge, contained by the higher retaining walls, never washed over the dock offices. The floating docks, with their properly tied off boats, rode high on the new pilings but never reached the top. The new tie-up policies, strictly adhered to by the club's members, prevented all but minor damage. It appeared that the cost in time and preparation had paid off for Seapath Yacht Club.

Then on September 14, 2005, Hurricane Ophelia, dragging her feet as one of the slowest-moving storms in history, pummeled the club for almost 2 days. The surge rose to within inches of the top of the retaining walls, yet they held perfectly. Almost no boats were damaged, again due to the upgraded construction and thorough preparation prior to the storm.

Seapath Yacht Club learned its lessons—some of them the hard way. Now it has a well-honed plan for storm preparation, which includes distributing the following boat-preparation instructions to every slip owner in the club:

The following procedure should be followed when preparing for a hurricane. These precautions must be made once a "hurricane watch" has been set for this area. You should plan to make these preparations yourself. If it appears that you are not taking the proper steps to protect your boat, which also insures the welfare of your neighbor's boat, then the marina staff will do them at your expense.

You must contact the marina within 2 hours of a "hurricane watch" being set if you plan to secure your own vessel, otherwise the marina staff will start the preparation process.

The steps you must follow are:

1. **Moor your boat in the slip with the stern toward the dock.** With the bow between the pilings, it allows the boat to have more room to move side to side without hitting the pilings. It also allows you to have more scope on your lines, which prevents the need for excess slack in the lines.

2. **Remove all sail and canvas.** The majority of the damage to boats during Hurricane Bertha and the March 1993 storm was due to the fact that self-furling headsails were not secured properly. Self-furling sails should be removed completely or a least secured with line from the top of the sail down. Once a headsail blows out it causes the boat to heel over, and in one case, the mast of a sailboat whose sail blew out hit the flybridge of the power-boat next to it. All canvas should be removed including full enclosures.

3. **Double all lines and put chafing gear where lines touch each other or run through a chock.** Lines should be of adequate size for the boat. Vessels up to 27 feet should have at least ⅜-inch nylon lines. Boats 27 to 38 feet long should have ½-inch lines, and vessels up to 55 feet should have ⅝-inch lines. Run your second line as you did the main line. It should be the same size, tension, and direction as the main line. [Author's comment: I disagree with this item, and recommend that the second line lead to a different tie-up location than the first.] The pur-pose of the second line is to help take the strain of the wind and act as a backup in case one line chafes. The second line helps to limit line stretch. Leave extra dock lines in the cockpit.

4. **Moor the boat as far away from the dock as possible to allow for line stretch.** Even though you have doubled your spring lines, the force of the wind will cause nylon lines to stretch. Secure your vessel far away from the dock to allow for that stretch. There should be at least 2 feet of clearance between your boat and any dock or piling when there is no wind blowing. You can readjust the lines after the storm to accommo-date boarding.

5. **Do not use eye splices to secure lines to boat or dock cleats.** A ready-made eye splice applied to a boat or dock cleat cannot be adjusted or removed under strain. If you belay your line at the dock and at the boat, marina staff can make required adjustments if necessary later.

6. **All lines that go from the boat to the floating dock should be taut.** When you leave slack in your lines, it allows the boat to swing wildly about in the slip. The momentum of the boat tugging against your lines will cause them to chafe more quickly, and puts more strain on your lines than if they have a constant strain on them. Because we have float-ing docks, there is no need to slacken lines to allow for a tidal surge. One bow line should be secured to the floating finger dock, the other bow line to the bow of the vessel next to you. This way all lines securing the vessel are secured to accommodate for tidal surge.

7. **Bow lines should be tied to pilings in the mid-tide range.** For those boats utilizing the pilings instead of the dock cleats, estimate the points

on your pilings where the bow cleat will be even in height at high and low tides. Place your bow line on the piling at a distance halfway between the highest and lowest points. Adjust the length of your bow lines with the bow cleats even with the height where your bow line is secured to the pilings. Your bow lines should be adjusted so your boat is held off the pilings in both directions. This should give you adequate scope for every situation and will keep your boat from banging into the pilings. Remember, you don't want your boat to be hanging from the cleats at low tide anymore than you want your boat straining on the lines at high tide.

8. **Tie your boat for what you know is going to happen instead of what may happen.** We have seen some boats tied with enough slack in their lines to accommodate a surge of 10 feet above normal high tide. When you leave that much slack in your lines, your boat will be bouncing off the pilings, which will cause damage to your boat and possibly break the pilings. Tie your lines without slack so that your boat will not pound against the pilings.

9. **Don't spiderweb your boat.** If you feel a need to spiderweb your boat as a preparation, then do so in the confines of your slip. When you stretch lines out and across the dock or across an adjoining slip, then it makes patrolling the docks more difficult and dangerous for marina staff and volunteer firefighters.

10. **Tie the tail end of a line to another cleat as a backup.** If you use a long enough stern line or spring line, then you can secure the tail end of the line to an adjacent cleat as a backup cleat. Do not run your line across the dock to another cleat. The Wrightsville Beach Fire Department will send people around the premises during slack wind periods during hurricanes to insure that no boats have broken free or are taking on water. Lines strung across the dock can be dangerous to them at night since there is no power on at the marina, hence no lights.

11. **Secure all loose items.** Items such as chairs, steps, life rings, boat hooks, fender boards, dinghies, and spare fuel tanks should be secured by line or stowed below to prevent them from being blown around. Close all seacocks. Close engine fuel valves at the tank. Shut off propane tanks at the tank. Secure wind generators and remove fans if possible.

12. **Where you may moor.** Under no conditions will any vessel be allowed to stay on the south side of "A" dock during hurricane conditions. [This is the outside dock that faces in the normal storm direction.] Vessels docked on the south side of "A" dock will be allowed to move inside the marina if space is available. Vessels on the north side of "A" dock are

encouraged to move to another location and will be moved by the
marina staff if space is available elsewhere.

Although the Seapath guidelines contain quite a bit of localized information, they
offer many valuable ideas gleaned from the Club's experience. See Appendix C for
Seapath Yacht Club's complete hurricane policy, including the preparations made by
the staff to secure the facility. By seeing the scope and scale of the staff's responsibilities, you will better understand the need to cooperate with marina staff and take personal responsibility for preparing your own boat.

See Appendix B for a hurricane preparedness checklist developed by FEMA and
the U.S. Coast Guard, and see Appendix D for the storm-preparation checklist of
Brewer Cove Haven Marina in Barrington, Rhode Island. It's interesting to note how
the policies of this commercial marina in the Northeast differ from those of the boataminium in the Southeast.

6

Tracking a Storm

We have looked at hurricanes, tornadoes, thunderstorms, nor'easters, and regional winds. We have learned about their causes and effects, where they develop, and where they can strike. Now let's take a look at how we can get storm information that will help us keep track of developing weather situations.

Through a complicated network of weather stations, buoys, satellites, and hurricane hunter aircraft, as well as government, academic, and private observations, a vast amount of weather information is gathered on a daily, even hourly, basis. These millions of pieces of data are then analyzed by weather experts at universities such as Dr. Bill Gray at Colorado State University, and government agencies such as the National Oceanic and Atmospheric Agency (NOAA) and the National Hurricane Center (NHC).

Each of these institutions uses computers that have made forecasting somewhat easier yet more prone to conflicting opinions. For hurricane analysis, there are presently six widely used computer models that analyze inputted information and spit out projected paths and forecasts. Though the computer models use similar data, their projections often don't agree.

On some NOAA websites, when you look at maps of a hurricane's projected path you will see each model's latest projections overlaid one on the other. The NHC analyzes each of these computer models and then comes up with a single projected path, which they issue with an advisory. As you follow the progress of a storm, you will see a new advisory every few hours. A specific storm sometimes will have 20, 30, 40 or more advisories before it weakens and no longer requires updating. Many websites will display both a map and an advisory discussion.

A quick way to get a feel for a storm's progress is to look at the forecasted path on the site's map. The anticipated storm path will be shown as a cone (which actually looks more like a wedge) projected forward 3 days, with a different-colored cone projecting out 5 days. In both the 3- and 5-day projections, the wider cone of possibility shows the area the entire storm is expected to cover, and the narrower cone shows the area of highest wind and greater severity. The whole cone of possibility shows the

NOAA hurricane-hunter aircraft fly right into the eye of a hurricane to collect data such as wind speed, precipitation, and barometric pressure. This data is quickly incorporated into NOAA's storm prediction analysis. (Courtesy NOAA)

geographical area the storm might impact. This cone of possible strike locations gives you some idea of the potential changes in direction the storm might take using current data.

These data can alter suddenly and often do. The closer the storm gets to landfall, the more accurate the projections become. But keep in mind that these projections—accurate as they can seem—are only guesses; hurricanes are famous for making last-minute changes in course. As an example, on August 11, 2004, Hurricane Charley was projected to come ashore near Tampa/St. Petersburg, on the Gulf Coast of Florida, then head north into the interior. Mandatory evacuation orders sent thousands of people east to Atlantic coastal towns where they sought shelter. At the last minute, though, Hurricane Charley veered right and came ashore on Cayo Costa, just north of Captiva Island, then stormed across Florida to hit the very communities evacuees thought would be safe.

When you want detailed information on a storm, read the discussions in Internet weather advisories. Many are written by NOAA and NHC forecasters and contain a wealth of information. (See the Weather Online section below for specific website addresses.) Maximum sustained winds and minimum central barometric pressure are two reported pieces of data to monitor carefully. As a storm builds, the winds increase and the barometric pressure decreases. The advisory will also tell where the storm's center is located, what land areas are immediately threatened, how current weather conditions are affecting the storm, and lots of other information. It even gives the percentage chance that the center of a storm will pass within 75 miles of specific locations within the next 72 hours. Cities or islands will be identified along with a percentage of danger, even though they might seem too far away. The potential strike percentage is just one of the pieces of information I track when a storm is approaching. When I see it grow to over 10 percent for my city of Wilmington, North Carolina, I begin to take the storm very seriously.

I may be a bit paranoid about hurricanes, but I live on a vulnerable East Coast shoreline. My media watch begins in late May every year and doesn't relax until the beginning of November. Most of my boating friends have similar media priorities. On an almost daily basis, I follow Internet websites specifically designed to track and assess tropical cyclones. These Internet sites, such as the many NOAA sites, begin tracking suspicious weather systems, such as easterly waves and developing low-pressure areas, well before they coalesce into threatening storms. It is a rare occasion when weather forecasts only give the bare minimum of a 1- to 2-day early warning. (I describe my favorite Internet sites in this chapter and list them more concisely in Appendix A.)

When the storm is about 36 hours away, I add TV's Weather Channel and CNN to my media schedule. Though their information is not as complete and may not be as up-to-date as the NOAA websites, they assign journalists to physically cover the likely impact areas early in the game. Their reporting often tends to be overly alarmist, but they provide interesting on-the-spot coverage. In 2004, I tuned in to CNN and watched a journalist broadcasting from the deck of a house just a few doors down from mine at North Topsail Beach, North Carolina. The raging ocean scene behind him told even more than his shocking report.

I also begin watching my local TV station for community advisories, such as bridge closings, voluntary or mandatory evacuations, and shelter locations. But I don't rely on local TV storm reports, as they are often late with storm development updates. Useful weather advisories are rarely given on an hourly basis, which is what I need to put my plan into action.

When the storm is approximately 12 hours away, I begin listening to local radio, which by this point will have up-to-the-minute live coverage and advisories.

By following a storm using the Internet, television, and local radio, you should be able to get a good fix on the predicted severity of the storm, as well as when and where it should strike.

But throughout all of this, don't lose sight of the fact that a power failure will almost inevitably occur. With a loss of power, you will lose the computer, television, and radio connections (unless you have a generator). You have a better chance of staying in touch with media announcements if you have a battery-powered radio and

NOAA Weather Radio Broadcasts	
BROADCAST CHANNEL	**FREQUENCY (MHz)**
WX1	162.550
WX2	162.400
WX3	162.475
WX4	162.425
WX5	162.450
WX6	162.500
WX7	162.525

Source: NOAA

a laptop computer that can still connect through your phone line, if phone service remains functioning. Keeping the laptop fully charged during hurricane season is a task for your list of seasonal chores (see Chapter 5). Even if you have an operational laptop, your connection to the Internet through cable or satellite can conceivably be lost during a storm. In this age of high-tech communication, a simple battery-operated portable radio or the car's radio may be the best, or even the only, connection with weather advisories and community emergency information.

NOAA Weather Radio should certainly be one of your sources for up-to-the-minute forecasts. NOAA broadcasts local marine and general forecasts continually on the frequencies shown in the table above. Some general-purpose portable radios and most VHF radios can receive these frequencies. More convenient may be the small, inexpensive, battery-powered weather radios that only receive the NOAA broadcast channels. Some weather radios automatically search for the strongest signal. Others require that you switch manually from station to station, but with a maximum of seven available preset frequencies, it's easy to find the nearest station putting out the strongest signal. Consider adding a weather radio to your preparedness kit.

Satellite radio is also well worth considering. You can stay in touch with the world when power lines are down by using satellite radio boom boxes, portable handsets, or car attachments. With hardware costs in the range of $100 and monthly subscription fees of under $15, satellite radio offers a host of national news networks and weather stations, though their reception may be affected by the storm.

Then there is a wireless Internet card that, when installed in your laptop computer, allows you to connect to the Web via the nearest cellular phone tower. As of this writing, the available cards are not very fast but will, at least, allow you to access Internet weather sites and give you a way to stay in touch with worried family members who might be far away. Cellular functionality during or after a storm is not guaranteed, but it may offer an alternative means of making a connection if landline services are down.

There are a host of other government weather products that are geared toward the needs of mariners at sea—especially commercial mariners. These include teletype over radio, weather faxes, e-mail services, medium- and high-frequency radio voice broadcasts, and others. If you plan to cross oceans, they are worth looking into, but for the typical boatowner, these are complicated, often expensive, and probably unnecessary. An excellent discussion of these resources, as well as an almost exhaustive treatise on hurricane preparedness in the North Atlantic Basin, can be found in the "Mariner's Guide for Hurricane Awareness in the North Atlantic Basin," which may be downloaded from the National Weather Service website (www.nhc.noaa.gov/HAW2/pdf/marinersguide.pdf).

TRACK IT YOURSELF

Though many of the websites described in this section track the progress of hurricanes in very nearly real time, you may want to keep your own records.

First you will need a blank chart of the Atlantic or Pacific ocean. Go to the NHC website (www.nhc.noaa.gov) and at the bottom of the home page choose a downloadable blank tracking chart for your region (see example, opposite). These charts have longitude and latitude grids on which you can pencil in a storm's progress. Enter the data you wish from the varied sources at your disposal.

WEATHER ONLINE

Choosing weather websites can be like going into the bookstore and not knowing which book you want. There are hundreds of weather sites, and scrolling around one usually leads you to numerous others through links. Many sites have infrared, visuals, moisture content, and other satellite maps that show the storm in real time and graphic detail. Others have lengthy advisories and discussions that give thorough scientific information about the development of the storm, its category, warnings for specific locations, and much more. Some have maps that show the storm track and its projected path.

As you find weather websites that you like, I suggest you store them as Favorites on your computer browser under a category such as Weather, so you can go back to them again and again to watch the progress of the storm. You can jump from one favorite to the next to see, for example, the projected track on website A, satellite imagery on website B, and a full-text advisory on website C.

Friends call me quite often to say they have discovered a new site that they like. But following up on all of them is an almost endless task as sites continue to come

Atlantic Basin Hurricane Tracking Chart
National Hurricane Center, Miami, Florida

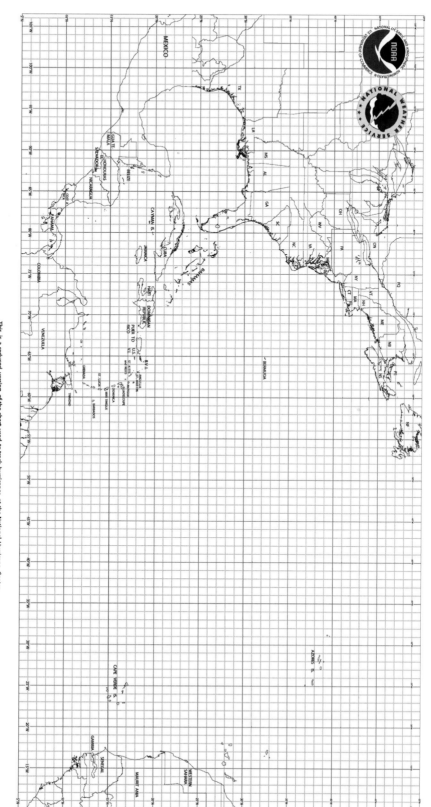

This is a reduced version of the chart used to track hurricanes at the National Hurricane Center

Using a chart to keep track of a storm's progress will keep you intimately involved in the process. This one is available as a download from the National Hurricane Center. (Courtesy NOAA/NHC)

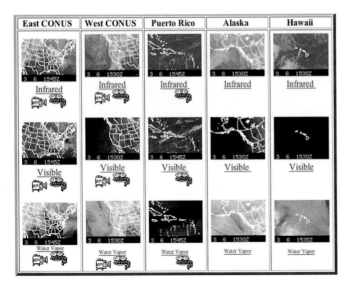

This screen capture shows the different current satellite images offered at www.goes.noaa.gov. (Courtesy NOAA)

and go. However, there are a number of websites that I highly recommend. Take a look at them and see if they meet your needs, and follow the links to other sites; you may find some new favorites that are not included here.

Severe Weather Websites

National Oceanic and Atmospheric Administration (NOAA), Geostationary Satellite Server, www.goes .noaa.gov. This is the granddaddy of all satellite sites. This address will take you to their satellite server, the main federal site for marine interests, with many subsites (see example). On the menu on the left side there are two particularly useful topic areas: Tropical Atlantic/Pacific covers the Atlantic, Pacific, Gulf of Mexico, and East Coast satellite imagery; and Severe Storm Sectors covers all severe events. Once you have found these subsites, save them as favorites for next time.

National Hurricane Center, www.nhc.noaa.gov. Run by NOAA, the National Hurricane Center in Miami, Florida, will probably be your main source for general storm information, comprehensive overviews, discussions, imagery, and advisories of active storms. During the hurricane/typhoon season, click on the Tropical Weather Discussion link under Atlantic—Caribbean Sea—Gulf of Mexico or Eastern Pacific. You will be presented with a block of choices for each named or numerical storm. Click on Public Advisory or Forecast Advisory to read details of the storm's intensity, position, direction, and areas subject to warning. Click on Discussion for the detailed reasoning behind the forecaster's predictions. This is where serious weather hobbyists can deepen their understanding of how storms and storm forecasting work. You can also look at maps and charts. Of particular interest are the maps of wind speed probabilities, the 3- and 5-day tracking cones, and the wind swath.

For a summary of marine safety and hurricanes, go to www.nhc.noaa.gov/HAW2/ english/marine_safety.shtml.

National Weather Service, Interactive Weather Information Network, http://iwin.nws.noaa.gov. This site gives detailed worldwide, regional, or city-specific advisories. Click on either the Animated or Enhanced Graphics version, depending on your Internet connection speed. To obtain local weather, click on Animated Graphics, Local Weather, your state, then your city to display a 24-hour summary and current

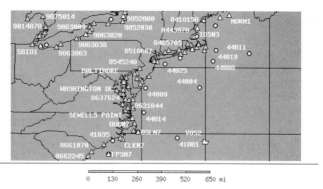

conditions. Also, click on National Warnings, and you'll get several options, including hurricanes, tornadoes, severe thunderstorms, and flooding, with written advisories on these weather events (if active) throughout the United States.

NOAA Satellite and Information Service, Operational Significant Event Imagery, www.osei.noaa.gov. This site has unusual satellite imagery of volcanoes, hurricanes, fires, dust storms, floods, and icebergs. Click on Tropical Cyclones, Hurricanes, & Typhoons for hurricane imagery or click on Severe Weather.

○ NWS NOOS Moored Buoy
△ NWS NOOS Coastal-Marine Automated Network (C-MAN)
☆ NWS NOOS Deep-Ocean Assessment and Reporting of Tsunamis (DART)
⌂ NWS NOOS Voluntary Observing Ship (VOS) Program
△ NOS National Water Level Observation Network (NWLON)
▲ NOS Physical Oceanographic Real-Time System (PORTS)
■ TMB Pilot Research Moored Array, Tropical Atlantic (PIRATA)
◉ TMB Tropical Atmosphere Ocean/Triangle Trans-Ocean Buoy Network (TAO/TRITON)

National Data Buoy Center, www.ndbc.noaa.gov. NDBC provides detailed weather information gathered from buoys located along the coast and

At www.ndbc.noaa.gov you can click on the sea buoy of your choice to get wave height, wind speed, and more. (Courtesy NOAA)

offshore. This site is so popular that it gets up to a million hits a month. Click on an area of the world and then the number of the buoy you're interested in. You'll get details of wind direction, wind speed and gusts, wave height, swell, air temperature, water temperature, and sea level pressure. It's an easy way to get fishing or cruise information from buoys stationed at or near your destination or route. Knowing the conditions far down the coast or way out to sea has saved many a fisherman trip, and gives storm watchers another tool in their arsenal. You can information over your cell phone by calling Dial-A-Buoy at 228-688- the phone keypad to give the buoy identifier number (once you've buoys of interest, by number, from the website).

of Hawaii, Tropical Storms, Worldwide, www.solar.ifa.hawaii.edu/ on Atlantic Ocean under the GIF Storm Track Maps category and large map covering the full Atlantic Ocean with a track of all active storms, which you can easily follow. I often open this one first just to see what weather situation has popped up during the last 24 hours.

The Weather Underground, www.wunderground.com/tropical. This location on this site gives good tropical storm advisories and local storm information. Take a look at Satellite Imagery, then Atlantic visible to see the subject tropical cyclone in action.

Unisys Weather, www.weather.unisys.com/hurricane. At this site you'll find current storm data plus hurricane statistics for any previous year. Go to your region of interest (e.g., Atlantic, East Pacific, etc.), select a year, and you will find a map

with tracks of all hurricanes of that year. There are also individual storm maps and details. This is a great site to help you settle disagreements about past storms.

Intellicast Weather, www.intellicast.com. This is a fairly commercial site, but it has an easily navigated index of U.S. storms, including severe storms, tropical storms, and winter storms, as well as radar and satellite images. During hurricane season, click on Hurricanes to get a quick update on active storms. An unusual feature can be found under Planners, where you can find areas of the country that are rated from great to poor for sports such as golf, sailing, skiing, and traveling.

Caribbean Weather Information, www.caribwx.com. This is a favorite of mine, and one that is cherished by boaters in the Caribbean. Stationed on the island of Tortola, British West Indies, the talented staff gives accurate storm forecasting for the Caribbean. Though the site gives mostly localized information, it provides a close look at storms that may well strike the United States mainland a day or two later. Click on Synopsis to get a view of Caribbean weather in general. Click on Hurricanes to view a fresh approach at reporting severe weather.

Tropical Ecosystems, http://jrscience.wcp.muohio.edu. R. Hays Cummins at Miami University in Ohio has an incredible website that includes links to many of the above sites as well as dozens of others. Cummins's site is the closest one to being all inclusive that you will probably find. Even if you save no other sites to your favorites list than the NOAA sites, you should add this one. During hurricane season, as you scroll down, there are active displays of maps, radar, satellite images, and forecasts from many of the severe weather sites I have already mentioned. This means you don't have to keep opening and closing sites or searching through links to get the whole story. They are already displayed here.

Once you get to Cummins's master site, scroll down to Environmental Links: Weather & Earth Science Resources. During severe weather situations and hurricane season, click on Radar and Severe Weather to see at least 15 U.S. maps of current weather. Or click on Hurricanes & Tropical Weather to view more maps, charts, and links than you could possibly

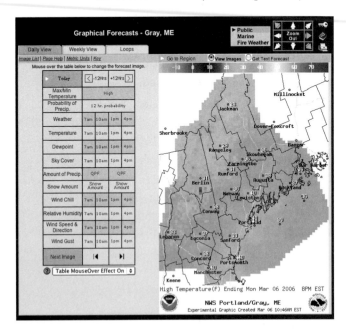

This National Weather Service site (www.srh.noaa.gov) features a great interactive page that allows you to call up almost any weather condition you might want. (Courtesy NOAA/NWS)

absorb in hours of study. Either subsite will take you to extensive selections of active satellite views and data on current severe weather. Some of his links may not be up to date; if you can't connect to a specific site, try entering its name into Google and see if an updated address is available. (This will work with any website you are having trouble logging onto.)

University of Wisconsin Cooperative Institute for Meteorological Satellite Studies, http://cimss.ssec.wisc.edu. Under Operational Satellites, click on Tropical Storms, then choose a region of the world you are interested in from the menu on the left. Click on Images and Movies under Global Mosaics to see moving images of weather activity.

Crown Weather Services, www.crownweather.com. This amateur site is a collection of dozens of great images and views of any part of the globe. Click on Tropical Weather Information and you'll get a rich variety of information. First you'll come to a written advisory; then scroll down to Infrared Images; then scroll down to the Surface Weather Analysis map that shows highs, lows, and tropical waves for the entire region; and last, scroll down to interesting upper-level wind maps at varying millibar levels.

Southern Regional Climate Center, www.srcc.lsu.edu. The Southern Regional Climate Center offers weather information throughout the South by region. Click on Tropical Desk under the Navigation menu. This site should be of particular interest to Gulf Coast residents.

Local Weather Websites

As a storm approaches you will need to bring your view in closer. There are a number of Internet websites that will give you local weather by typing in your zip code or county. Regional radar images at these sites often tell a very comprehensive local story. And don't forget local radio and television stations. They are where you will hear about bridge closings, areas of flooding, mandatory evacuation announcements, and storm shelter locations. However, don't depend on these local stations for the most recent weather advisories, as they are usually later in reporting compared to the frequent updates from the big boys.

National Weather Service, Southern Region Headquarters, www.srh.noaa.gov. This is a good place to check for local weather anywhere in the United States. Enter your local zip code and click Go to receive your local 5-day local forecast.

An interesting new addition is an experimental option on ways to analyze forecasts. Once you have brought up your local map, go to bottom of the page for Experimental Forecast Images (this is not available in every state; if you don't see it, look for the National Digital Forecast Database instead). Click on one of the maps, and it will take you to a new page. Move your cursor over the titles in the table on the left, and the forecast image on the right will refresh to show each subject (e.g., Temperature at 2 A.M., or Wind Speed and Direction at 7 P.M., 10 P.M., and 1 A.M.).

Accuweather, www.accuweather.com. This commercial site provides long-range forecasts of up to 15 days based on zip code entries.

The Weather Underground, www.wunderground.com. This site provides a good zip code 5-day forecast, past weather history, astronomy information, moon phases, and a long list of reports from personal weather stations.

National Ocean Service, Center for Operational Oceanographic Products and Services, www.tidesandcurrents.noaa.gov. Tide and current predictions are available here for your local area. From the dropdown menu under Products, select Predictions, then Published Tide Tables, and then the current year. Then choose your state and the location closest to your boat. If you then click on the Predictions column to the right, you will see month by month prediction times and tide heights. As you know, hurricanes that make landfall at high tide are much more likely to cause severe flooding and surge damage than those that hit at low tide.

When storms are forecast, if you click on Tides Online on the home page, then Storm Tide ALERT, then Water Level, you will see present and predicted water levels, wind speed and air/water temperatures. Each of these phenomena are critical ingredients for a storm surge.

For Weather Buffs

Here are a few rather esoteric sites that real weather buffs and aficionados might like to investigate for specific weather-related information.

University College London, Seasonal Weather Forecasts, http://forecast.mssl.ucl.ac.uk. This site gives a European look at worldwide weather patterns.

U.S. Geological Survey Center for Coastal & Watershed Studies, http://coastal.er.usgs.gov. Here you can find impact studies of recent hurricanes that show dramatic before-and-after aerial photographs of storm damage.

Federal Emergency Management Agency, www.fema.gov. Provides a broad look at past disasters and top stories about storms in the United States.

National Aeronautics and Space Administration, www.nasa.gov. NASA takes you on an exciting trip to the stars, our planets, and faraway space views of severe weather. After opening this site, click on Skip to NASA Home Page. I guarantee that you won't be able to resist looking at their sensational photographs and videos.

U.S. Army Corps of Engineers, www.usace.army.mil. Here you'll find information about flood control, disaster relief, and many other subjects.

EARTHQUAKES ONLINE

Earthquakes are not covered elsewhere in this book since very few boats have any likelihood of being damaged by one, and earthquakes are not really "weather" in any case. On the other hand, earthquakes can generate tsunamis, which have enough similarities to a hurricane's storm surge that some boatowners might well consider them closely related threats. I'm sure that if I stored my boat in an earthquake-prone area, they'd be right up there on my worry list.

U.S. Geological Survey, Earthquake Hazards Program, 24-Hour Aftershock Forecast Map, http://pasadena.wr.usgs. gov/step. This site calculates the probability of strong ground-shaking events at specific locations over a 24-hour period. Matthew Gerstenberger, who developed the site, said that the forecast maps would be most useful to predict aftershocks once a temblor (earthquake) that was strong enough to break windows and crack plaster had hit. Previously, residents were able to quickly view real-time earthquake maps with the click of a mouse. But even though those maps were posted and updated within minutes after a temblor occurred, they did little to warn people ahead of time. Since aftershocks are likely, now residents can use this website to click on real-time, color-coded maps that provide earthquake aftershock probabilities for a specific

region. Areas shaded in red represent a high chance of strong shaking within the next 24 hours, while those in blue represent a very remote chance.

Duncan Agnew of the Scripps Institution of Oceanography at the University of California, San Diego, commented that these new forecast maps give earthquake victims a "much more precise answer" about the risk of aftershocks after a strong tremor.

U.S. Geological Survey, Earthquake Hazards Program, Northern California, http://quake.wr.usgs.gov. This site contains a daily earthquake forecast website that is reportedly updated hourly. Click on California-Nevada under Real Time Earthquake Maps on the left-hand menu to see a map of California showing all the projected hot spots.

PROTECTING YOUR BOAT FROM AN EARTHQUAKE

Measures to protect your boat from an earthquake differ little from those for storm disasters. Land-stored boats will be the most affected, so double up on jack stands. If at all possible, remove boats from lifts and dry-stack storage and place them either on trailers or on the ground. If your boat is in the water, prepare it as you would for a storm surge by securing it with doubled lines in every direction. If you're on a mooring or at anchor, let out as much scope as possible, and make sure that your ground tackle is solid and sound.

Keep in mind that road and bridge disruptions will be inevitable after an earthquake, causing delays or making it impossible to get to your boat.

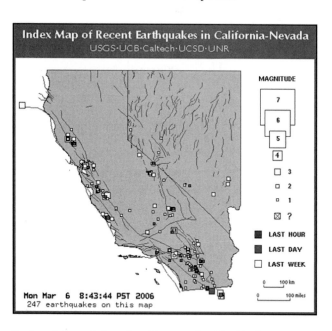

Earthquakes aren't "weather," but you should still take steps to protect your boat from their effects. If you live in California, go to http://quake.wr.usgs.gov for predictions. (Courtesy USGS)

7 Shelter from the Storm: Where to Leave Your Boat

Choosing the right place for your boat prior to a storm is difficult. Part of the problem is deciding when to put your plan into action—too soon may be almost as troublesome as too late. If you move the boat to your chosen hurricane hole or trailer it to your home before the storm's landfall is certain, you may move the boat directly into the path of the storm.

The other part of the problem is that no single location is best for all storm scenarios—you never know exactly what direction the wind will come from, the height of the storm surge, the amount of inland flooding, or about a dozen other variables. You can and should, however, gather all the information you can, make your best guesses on the nature of the threat, and act accordingly.

As the hurricane experts begin issuing 3-day and then 1-day forecasts, the nail-biting begins in earnest. Usually, within 24 hours of landfall the weather forecasters have identified the impact area quite accurately, although there is no way to be absolutely sure of a storm's impact area until it actually hits. There are many instances of storms veering only a few hours before hitting land. In 2005, Hurricane Katrina aimed directly at New Orleans, then shifted slightly to the east and made landfall in Mississippi. This subtle shift saved the city from a direct hit, although the storm-related flooding after Katrina had passed was devastating.

Somewhere between 36 and 48 hours prior to the storm's landfall, based on the best information available to you, you will have to decide whether to move or not, and then implement your plans in a deliberate manner, not a last-minute mad scramble.

Expected wind direction is one of the many pieces of information to be concerned about. Once you have a good fix on where the eye will hit, you will know the direction you can expect the wind to come from and its potential intensity at your boat's location.

Remember, a hurricane is a swirling mass of high winds spinning counterclockwise with an eye in the center. The upper-right quadrant will have the highest wind speeds. The farther to the left or right of the eye you are, the less dramatic the wind shifts will be.

Hurricanes traveling along the Atlantic coast of the United States have a general north-south orientation; those in the Gulf Coast generally have an east-west orientation. In both regions, hurricanes usually approach from somewhere between an easterly and a southerly direction. (Occasionally, however, a maverick will fool everyone.)

Examine the history of previous storms in your region and establish the most common direction of a storm's approach and its wind direction when it hits. Previous storms may have also left a pattern of how storm surge affected your particular area. Hurricanes are not students of history, and there will always be surprises, but knowing past behaviors will get you thinking more clearly about how to prepare.

If you experience a direct hit by the eye, the direction of the wind will move in a clockwise direction a full 360 degrees, essentially ending up blowing from the same direction where it began. This is the most difficult scenario to protect against, not only because you have to secure your boat against the winds coming from all directions but also because of the increased chances that damage to nearby boats and structures will impact your boat regardless of how carefully you prepare it. Fortunately, the chances of being hit directly by the eye are small, as the eye is usually no more than 10 to 15 miles across.

If you are not hit directly by the eye, you will probably experience no more than a 90-degree wind shift. This makes it much easier to decide whether to move to a different location or hunker down at your marina. Few marinas—and few anchorages of any sort—offer good 360-degree protection, but it's not too hard to find an area protected from winds coming from just one or two quadrants of the compass.

First, try to determine if you will be on the strong side or the weak side of the storm. If you live on the East Coast and the storm is moving west, then north of the eye will experience the strongest winds and south of the eye the weakest. If you're on the Gulf Coast and the storm is moving north, then the weak side is to the west of the eye, and the strong side to its east. Another way to look at this is, if you face in the direction the storm is heading, your right arm will point to the strongest area of the storm, your left arm to the weakest part of the storm.

Remember that the storm's strong side will also have the greatest storm surge: the range from extreme low water to the top of a storm surge that is coming on top of a high tide can be 20 feet or more. The weak side, on the other hand, might or might not experience storm surge (which, in any case, would probably be lower than on the strong side), and could even experience tides much lower than normal.

Once you know where the storm's eye will strike, you can implement your plan A—to stay put and fortify your position or plan B—to move elsewhere.

CHOOSING THE BEST SITUATION

Your options are few, and are easily divided into in-the-water and out-of-the-water choices. Your in-the-water options are to anchor or moor your boat in your regular harbor or a preselected hurricane hole that offers better protection; keep it tied up at a slip or dock; or move it to the middle of a narrow creek or canal and secure it with a combination of anchors and dock lines to shore.

As for out-of-the-water options, the only dry-storage option available for a larger boat is putting it on jack stands or in a cradle at the marina. If you have a smaller boat, you can also store it on a rack in a dry-stack marina, on davits or lifts, on a trailer, or possibly right on the ground (depending on its hull shape) either in a boat-yard or at home.

Each storage scenario involves weighing the various pros and cons, such as cost and complexity of each arrangement, potential threats versus differing levels of safety of each choice, etc. The table summarizes several key considerations, each of which is described in greater detail below.

A study by the Massachusetts Institute of Technology (MIT) after Hurricane Gloria (1985) found that boats stored on shore were more likely to survive a severe storm than those stored in the water. I believe that many of those boats the study found damaged in the water would have fared better had their owners followed better protective measures. But since the MIT study was both empirically sound and well

Storage Choices for Hurricanes and Severe Storms

	IN THE WATER				ON LAND			
	Mooring	Anchor	Slip/ Dock	Canal or Creek	Dry Stack	Jack Stands or Cradle	Davits or Lift	On a Trailer/On the Ground
Large-boat option?	yes	yes	yes	yes	no	yes	no	no
A "stay-put" option for many boaters?	yes	unlikely	yes	yes	yes	only if boat is already out of the water	yes	yes
Subject to storm surge and/or waves?	yes	yes	yes	yes	depends on location	depends on location	yes	depends on location
Intensity of storm pre-parations (time and/or expense)	moderate	high	moderate	moderate to high	low	moderate to high	low	low to moderate

disseminated, it warrants careful consideration. You may find that your marina, as part of its hurricane plan, has a plan for hauling as many boats as possible prior to a storm. But don't take the marina's plan for granted, and don't assume that your plan is understood. Whether you plan to pull the boat, leave it in your slip or on your mooring, or clear out altogether, clarify your plans with marina management at the beginning of the season. And contact them to make specific arrangements as soon as a storm warning is issued. If, for example, your plan A is to stay put, but based on a storm's particular approach, you decide to go to plan B and move your boat to a different location, be sure to tell the marina staff what you're doing; it will save them a lot of time and stress after the storm when they notice your boat is missing.

IN-THE-WATER STORAGE

If storage in the water is your choice, it is essential that your boat be in a protected harbor and not one that is overly vulnerable to storm surge and high winds. This is a decision that can be made months before the storm season begins. In choosing a safe harbor, there are a number of parameters to consider.

It is preferable to be located on a windward shore that is not perpendicular to the coastline. In other words, try to choose a harbor anchorage or docking arrangement where the wind and waves cannot bear down on your boat after getting a long run over open water. If you are in an anchorage or marina that is on a downwind or lee shore in a bay or inlet perpendicular to the coastline, you may be overly exposed. If your present site is vulnerable, you should identify a windward shore location that is not perpendicular to the coast, and close enough to get to within the limited amount of time you'll likely have once a storm warning is issued.

Remember that accurate strike information is often not available until just 24 hours before landfall, and by then the weather will probably have begun to deteriorate. Moving to a safer location early, while the weather is still good, makes a great deal of sense. Of course, it is preferable to move the boat during daylight hours than at night.

Even if your boat is on a mooring in a well-protected harbor, it may still seem more exposed to the storm than one snugged down tightly in a slip. But there are some advantages to being on a mooring. A boat on a mooring will swing and always face into the wind. This is the least vulnerable position because it presents the smallest amount of windage, the smallest profile subject to battering waves, and—in the case of an open boat—the smallest odds of swamping. Although boats on a mooring and at anchor have a high rate of loss because of dragging anchors and failed ground tackle, these problems can be addressed (see below and Chapter 9). If your gear is in excellent condition, your boat will probably survive intact.

Mooring fields tend to be densely packed to accommodate the greatest possible number of boats in a limited space while also allowing each boat a reasonable amount

This boat in a channel near Wrightsville Beach, North Carolina, is anchored off a soft shore with two bow anchor lines and one stern anchor line. The owner is counting on the strong current to align the boat fore and aft, but at the risk of storm winds from an east-moving storm hitting it broadside.

The benefits of a soft shore downwind made manifest. Even though this boat came adrift during Hurricane Dennis (July 16, 2005), it likely sustained little damage since it grounded on Pensacola Beach. (Courtesy FEMA)

of scope appropriate for normal weather conditions. In storm conditions, however, each boat should have longer scope. In some anchorages, this is accomplished by thinning out the field—pulling some boats out of the water or requiring some of them to relocate. But if this is not an option, you can add a second storm anchor, at a 45-degree angle to the primary mooring anchor, to allow you to let out a little more scope. This should keep your boat within a confined swinging arc.

What if your ground tackle fails? Well, you'll be driven ashore, but even there, you have choices. The best lee shores are sand beaches, mangroves, or swamps (never rocks or seawalls). If your boat breaks loose and grounds on a soft shore, damage will probably be light. If you expect a direct eye strike, anchoring on a windward shore with a soft beach to leeward of the storm's expected direction of movement may be the best alternative to the complexities of protecting your boat from a 180-degree wind shift while at a slip.

Anchoring in a Hurricane Hole

Hurricane holes are safe anchorages with bottoms of excellent holding ground, soft bottoms to leeward, and good protection from wind and waves. They are usually deep, narrow coves or inlets that are surrounded by sturdy trees that block the wind and provide tie-off points for lines. The best location for a hurricane hole is one far enough inland to avoid the most severe winds and storm surge yet close enough to reach at short notice. If you have to (or choose to) anchor your boat during a storm, you will want to find a hurricane hole. Scout out your location months before the season begins, as you may need to get permission from landowners to tie up to their trees.

Good holes can be popular and usually fill up quickly, so practice getting there, and make plans to do it early when a storm warning is announced. You should know the best route, how long it takes, and bridge-opening times (if needed). Bridges will undoubtedly be closed as the time of impact approaches to allow residents to evacuate. If you wait too long, your passage can be blocked.

For example, Miami-Dade County in Florida has a specific lockdown procedure that calls for all bridges to be closed 8 hours before the predicted landfall of a storm with winds 40 miles per hour or greater. This timing is announced by the Coast Guard at least 6 hours before implementation. Therefore, boaters who wish to move have at least 6 hours' warning before lockdown. But not all communities have such well-developed, publicized plans. In some areas, bridges may close with little or no advance notice.

Can you imagine the frustration—even panic—of arriving at a closed bridge and being unable to proceed to your hurricane hole? You may have no choice but to return to your regular slip or mooring. By the way, you *have* made preparations for your boat's survival *there* just in case, haven't you? Even if you do plan to get an early start toward your hurricane hole, it's a good idea to have a plan B to cover yourself for this scenario.

Another factor to consider in deciding on a potential hurricane hole is storm surge. A long line arrangement off a windward shore lets a boat rise to the height of the storm surge whereas at a dock even long lines can't always cope with the challenge of a huge surge.

Try to avoid bodies of water that are funnel shaped, with a narrow windward entrance opening to a wider anchorage inside. Strong winds can force water through the entrance and prevent the water from tributary rivers and streams from flowing out, causing the water to pile up and rise to unusual heights as the storm progresses. If the only hurricane hole available is in a funnel, be sure to have considerable scope out to deal with this pileup effect of storm surge. Also try to avoid anchoring downwind from other boats; their anchors might drag and the boats could come charging down on you with the current. See Chapter 9 for more on anchoring.

Many barrier islands offer dubious protection from storms. Most are quite low, offering little protection from the wind, and may be entirely over-washed in a severe storm.

Bottom Conditions for Anchoring

One of the most important factors in identifying your own personal hurricane hole is the nature of the bottom or holding ground. Depending on your budget and the amount of time available, you can either choose your holding ground to suit your anchors or select the anchors that are best suited to the best available holding ground. Marine stores tend to carry those types of anchors that work best in their local conditions—their advice may be invaluable.

J Nature of the Seabed

Types of Seabed		
Rocks → K		Supplementary national abbreviations: a–ag
1	S	Sand	S
2	M	Mud	M
3	Cy; Cl	Clay	Cy
4	Si	Silt	Si
5	St	Stones	St
6	G	Gravel	G
7	P	Pebbles	P
8	Cb	Cobbles	Cb
9	Rk; rky	Rock; Rocky	R
10	Co	Coral and Coralline algae	Co
11	Sh	Shells	Sh
12	S/M	Two layers, eg. Sand over mud	S/M
13.1	Wd	Weed (including Kelp)	Wd

Section J of Chart No. 1 will help you decipher abbreviations for bottom conditions—essential knowledge for finding good holding ground. (Courtesy *How to Read a Nautical Chart*/Nigel Calder and International Marine)

Sandy mud provides a good holding bottom. Hard sand is also good if you have the type of anchor that will dig into it. Soft mud or sand is not known for holding well. Rocks are problematic; many anchors simply won't set well in rocky bottoms. On the other hand, if your anchor does set well among rocks, it may set *too* well and be nearly impossible to break free after the storm. Avoid anchoring in grass if at all possible. Many anchors simply won't penetrate matted grasses, while others seem to take a set easily in grass even though they're not well dug in to the bottom and will pull out in a heavy blow.

Look at the chart that covers the area where you plan to anchor. It will show the basic bottom characteristics in abbreviations like "S" for sand, "M" for mud, "Cl" for clay, "Rk" for rocky, and "Wd" for weed. These and other common abbreviations are shown in Section J of Chart No. 1: Nautical Chart Symbols Abbreviations and Terms.

However, you will want more specific facts about the bottom than what's on the chart. The chart may say "sandy" throughout a harbor, but there may be patches of rock, grass, or mud. You need to know the bottom composition at the precise spot where you'll drop anchor. You have three options:

- Dive down and take a look.

- Drag a small anchor across the bottom and inspect any collected residue of mud or grass. If it comes up clean, you have confirmed an all-sand bottom. If the bottom is rocky, you can probably hear and feel it as you drag the anchor.

- Use an old-fashioned lead line with a hollow bottom filled with soft wax or hard grease to collect sediment. If nothing sticks, it's rocky down there.

Water depth is another consideration. The deeper the water, the longer your anchor rode must be to achieve the minimum recommended scope of 10:1. While storm surge may create very high water, necessitating an extremely long rode (and an extremely large swinging circle), there is also the possibility of extreme low water if wind and tide conditions combine to drag all the water out of your harbor. If this happens, you could find your boat sitting on the bottom—possibly on its side. So don't overlook the depth conditions as well as the bottom makeup of your harbor.

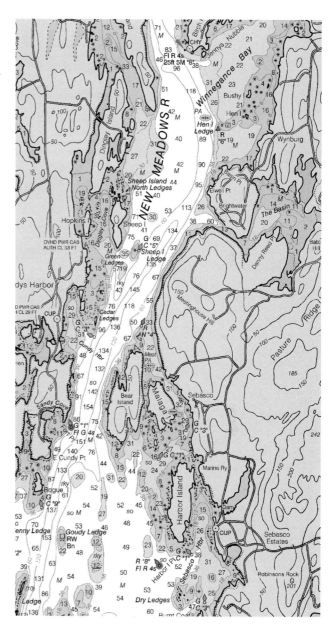

The nautical chart shows The Basin, a real hurricane hole up the New Meadows River in Maine.

If all else is satisfactory and you have a choice between deep water and more shallow water, choose the shallower site, as long as the depth is adequate to compensate for the possibility of extreme low water. Shallower water allows a better depth-to-length ratio and will provide better holding than the same length rode in deep water.

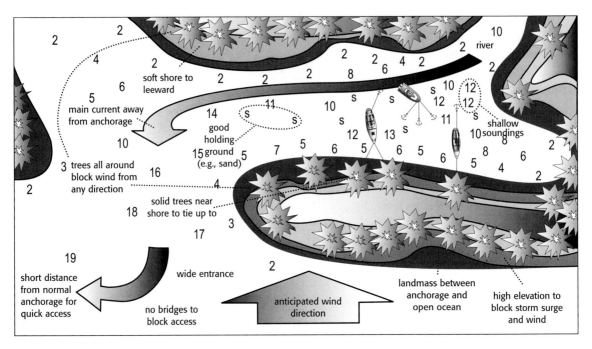

The idealized hurricane hole illustrated here will provide excellent storm protection. Among other virtues, it offers good holding ground in fairly shallow water; protection from wind, storm surge, and wave action; and a soft shore to leeward.

See the illustration above for an ideal hurricane hole; see Chapter 9 for more details on anchoring.

Tying Up at a Slip or Dock

Hurricane damage can be more severe for boats stored in boathouses or storage buildings than for boats in the water. Buildings are rigid and can be blown down whereas boats in a slip will ride with the tempest and not resist it.

A well-positioned and adequately constructed slip or dock can be a safe haven for a properly prepared boat. Floating concrete docks and concrete pilings are stronger than wooden ones but these are few and far between, and a wooden dock system will hold together fine if it is properly engineered and maintained. Pilings that secure floats should reach at least 12 to 14 feet above mean high water—even taller is even better. Ideally, the pilings should be higher than your gunwales at the maximum conceivable water level (with storm surge on top of a high tide).

Wide slips are better than narrow ones. There should be ample distance between the pilings or docks at your boat's widest point to allow the boat a certain amount of side-to-side movement in a storm. For example, if your boat has a 10-foot beam, there should be a minimum of 14 feet between the pilings. If the clearance is inadequate, no amount of fenders and lines will save your boat from a battering.

Speaking of fenders, they're really not much help if the boat is banging against the dock or piling, yet they are still worth putting out on the principle that every little bit may help. In fact, put out as many as you can, especially on the open-water side of the boat. They may give your vessel a little protection from a loose boat careening by.

If you have the option, try to get a berth that is not broadside to a potential storm's path. Once you have selected a slip that opens toward the expected wind, you should tie your boat so that the bow is facing into the storm's anticipated direction. Tying stern-to the wind will generally increase wind resistance and expose vulnerable doors, companionways, and engine exhausts. And while you will take additional measures to prevent water from entering through doors or into exhaust pipes (see Chapter 10), facing these away from the wind provides an excellent first line of defense. See Chapter 8 for more details on preparations in slips and at docks.

These steel-reinforced cement pilings are more than 14 feet high and will let the floating dock rise safely in the event of an exceptionally high storm surge.

Canals and Narrow Waterways

For those not familiar with Florida canals, these waterways define much of the coastal geography of southern Florida, providing a large proportion of the boat docking opportunities. Some

It wouldn't take much of a surge or high wind to damage the boat on the right, which is too wide for its berth.

are man-made cuts reaching inland from the shore, while others began as natural creeks or streams and were deepened and straightened artificially. In most cases, the sides are reinforced bulkheads, which are driven into the bottom so that boats can come right up to the wall yet still sit in deep water. In addition, concrete pylons may be driven against the bulkhead, and a floating dock added and held in place with pilings. Arrangements like this are found behind almost every home on the canals.

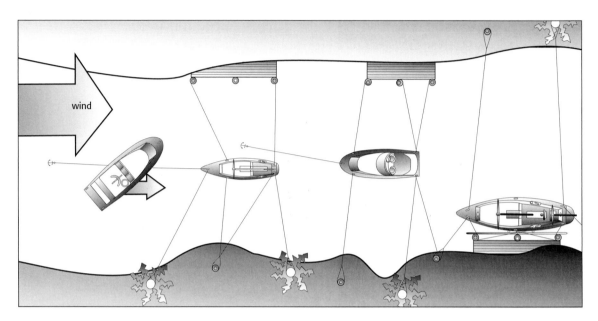

Canals can offer excellent protection from storm and wind and lots of good tie-off points, but boats can be at the mercy of a poorly secured boat that breaks free.

Such canals and other narrow waterways and creeks can provide good storm protection as long as they run roughly parallel to the coastline. Those that lie perpendicular to the coast and are open to the ocean can be hazardous since they are subject to direct wave and storm-surge hazards. Any boat that breaks free in such a canal will careen upstream, hitting boats along the way and causing a pileup at the end.

My friends Mark Griffis and David Robertson keep a 55-foot Sea Ray powerboat on a dock in the canal behind their home in Lighthouse Point, Florida. The canal is about 100 feet wide and at least 1 mile long. There are similar boats tied to similar docks all up and down the canal, which connects to many crossing canals, providing harbor to hundreds of boats. This situation is almost identical to thousands of others along the Florida coast and is particularly common in the Ft. Lauderdale area.

In a storm situation, the majority of the neighborhood's boatowners prefer to secure their boats in the middle of the canal, with the bows facing toward the probable wind direction and lines to each shore with enough scope to take the expected storm surge. (In the Lighthouse Point area, a big storm surge will often come 6 to 10 feet over the top of the seawall.)

However, there is a critical problem associated with this arrangement: the hundreds of boats that lie upstream of the ones already tied off to both shores. What if some of the boatowners living upstream—or even *one* of them—wants to leave the canal and seek a different storm refuge?

To prevent a Hatfield and McCoy–type battle, boatowners on narrow waterways have to reach a consensus plan for storm preparation. This may be arranged by a formal neighborhood organization, an e-mail list, flyers under front doors, or a scheduled neighborhood meeting, but everyone must be on the same page. This isn't something to try to accomplish when a storm warning is in effect—tensions will be running way too high for rational talk and compromise. Such community efforts must occur before the storm season begins.

On Mark and David's canal, everyone in the neighborhood has agreed that boaters who wish to leave must do so 2 days prior to the expected landfall. That gives the boatowners who plan to stay 2 days to secure their boats in the middle of the canal without worrying about someone upstream being trapped and unable to get out.

Diplomacy can go a long way in trying to enforce the neighborhood's decisions. Be flexible. Someone may have an absolutely compelling reason to anchor in "your" spot or to leave after the deadline, and if you can work with them, rather than opposing them, everything will go more smoothly. Approach your neighbor in a friendly and nonaggressive manner. Screaming at him for some infraction of the plan will only make it more difficult to correct the problem. Offer to help; it's much easier to run lines across a 100-foot-wide canal if you have some assistance. He may not have the knowledge or experience to make the best preparations. By helping him protect his boat, you will be adding to your own boat's safety.

But it seems there is always at least one absentee owner or a complacent person who will take no precautions. It is nerve-racking for canal residents to observe an uncared-for boat upwind of theirs—one that is all but certain to break loose and damage boats in its way. But it is not a good idea to take matters into your own hands and make what you feel are proper preparations for your neighbor's boat; you could subject yourself to potential legal liability, not to mention charges of trespassing. If you see a boat that is an accident waiting to happen, do everything you can to contact its owner and offer to help. If that doesn't work, all you can do is to place as many fenders as you can on the threatened side of your own boat and hope for the best.

One more arrangement bears mention. If your waterway is wide enough, you may be able to obtain a permit to drive pilings deep into the streambed so that your boat can be tied on both sides, fore and aft. This avoids the problem of blocking in boatowners upstream (at least by *your* boat), and the outer pilings will go a long way toward fending off any boats that break free. It will also make tying off much easier, since you won't be dealing with hundreds of feet of line. See Chapter 8 for more details on tying up effectively.

LAND STORAGE

Probably the safest option is to haul your boat and store it in a fully enclosed building rated for winds up to 145 miles per hour. If you can afford that, however, you can

The boats in this dry-stack storage area are not protected from flying debris.

This fully enclosed dry-storage facility offers good protection.

A CONTRARIAN OPINION

Ken Rohlman, a seasoned Florida captain, is a veteran of a dozen hurricanes, and he has seen, again and again, what works and what fails in Florida boatyards and canals.

Ken firmly believes that a boat is safer in the water than on land (although this contradicts the results of the MIT study mentioned earlier, which showed less damage for land-stored boats). Ken has observed that boats hauled and put in boatyards tend to suffer a great deal of damage from flying debris, while boats properly secured in the water survived all but the most catastrophic storms.

---

probably also afford to pay someone else to take care of *all* your storm preparations, and you don't need this book. So let's look at the on-land options that are available to us mere financial mortals.

Marina Land Storage

Hauling your boat and putting it on jack stands is one choice. At some marinas in some parts of the country, some boat-owners use cradles, which may provide better and more secure support than jack stands.

Before you decide, examine your marina's land storage area and practices, then compare the pros and cons of their facilities with those of remaining in the water. The storage area must be located high enough above sea level to avoid storm surge (or the prospect of inland flooding, if present). It's certainly not unknown for boats to be blown off their jack stands, so consider the area's general level of protection against the wind, as well as the care with which dry-storage preparations will be made. Just one poorly supported boat that tips off its stands can start a domino effect, toppling dozens of other boats downwind.

Some yards look more like construction sites, strewn with boards, ladders, sheds, paint cans, and other lightweight materials that can turn into flying debris and damage your boat. In-the-water storage is generally less vulnerable to this hazard.

Even with those possible drawbacks, many boaters prefer dry-land storage. On jack stands, your boat will either be subject to waves and storm surge or not, but there are no decisions to make about how to prepare the boat to deal with it. A jack stand is easier to inspect than a mooring and easier to deploy securely than an anchor. There are fewer lines to deal with, fewer knots to tie, and no fenders to deploy. Aside from the trouble of having the boat hauled, dry-land storage may be the easier option. And as the MIT study showed, there is evidence that it is safer overall.

Dry-Stack Storage

Dry-stack storage, while almost the norm for small-craft storage in some parts of the country, is almost unknown in others. Dry-stack racks may be wide open to the weather, covered by a roof and open on all four sides, or entirely enclosed within a (usually steel) building. Those that are not fully enclosed leave most of their boats quite vulnerable to high winds. Boats on the lowest level can be strapped down securely, but those on the second and higher levels generally have to rely on their weight alone to stay put. On the other hand, boats on the higher levels are generally above the height of a storm surge; those on the ground floor may be submerged. All boats in open dry-stack storage are susceptible to damage from wind-blown debris.

Many boat storage buildings aren't built to hurricane-rated standards and may not offer much protection. (Courtesy FEMA)

For boats in fully enclosed structures, the robustness of the building itself may be an issue. Conventionally engineered steel buildings can be torn apart by hurricane winds, posing an extreme hazard to the boats they are meant to protect. Some of the better dry-stack facilities use hurricane-rated structures.

Absent a fully enclosed, hurricane-rated building, dry-stack storage is probably not the safest option in a really powerful storm. However, this shouldn't cause too great an inconvenience for most owners since many boats in dry-stack storage are trailerable, and dry-stack facilities, such as those described below, have the equipment and the expertise to put your boat on its trailer with great efficiency.

Inlet Watch Yacht Club

Inlet Watch Yacht Club (www.inletwatch.com) in Wilmington, North Carolina, is a dry-stack marina located on the Intracoastal Waterway just across from a narrow, treeless barrier island of windswept sand and low vegetation. With approximately 400 dry-storage spaces, its forklifts run almost constantly, efficiently removing boats from their slots up to three levels high and depositing them beside the finger piers where their owners wait to take them out for an afternoon spin or for a shot at a plentiful run of bluefish. When they return, the forklifts pick the boat out of the water and deposit it on a work rack, where the owner can flush the engine with fresh water and clean the boat. Then the boat is returned to its parking place on the three-level stack.

The racks are built of solid concrete and rebar uprights, with concrete-covered steel I-beams for the horizontals. The marina's older structures have roofs, which assistant manager Darren Anderson feels are unnecessary. The roofs are a maintenance problem, attract nesting birds, and do little to protect the boats that are, for the most part, covered with canvas in normal weather. The marina's newer stacks are roofless.

Although some marinas stack boats up to five levels high, Inlet Watch has never gone higher than three levels; marina management has expressed reservations about the safety of additional tiers. Even a three-tier stack looks vulnerable to high winds, but Inlet Watch's wide-open architecture allows the wind to blow right through, minimizing the potential for damage to the structure.

As vulnerable as it sounds, Inlet Watch's dry-stack storage has been around for a long time, with some of its structures dating back to the 1980s. The marina has experienced a number of hurricanes with winds well over 100 miles per hour.

When Hurricane Fran hit as a Category 3 storm in September 1996, the dry-stack structures survived intact but almost all the boats stored on them were blown off and destroyed, or seriously damaged from flying debris. Just 3 years later, Hurricane Floyd cruised just offshore as a Category 5 storm, again causing heavy damage.

From these experiences, marina management realized that the most important advice they can give their clients is to have the most complete insurance coverage possible, and to keep it up to date. They also urge owners of trailerable boats to move them to a safer place.

When a hurricane watch is announced, Inlet Watch personnel begin hauling the boats in the basin and clearing the yard. Approximately 12 hours before the storm's projected landfall, all marina personnel are sent home to their families, except for a small crew who turn off the electricity and water and complete any last-minute jobs.

MarineMax

MarineMax (www.yachtworld.com/marinemaxcarolinas) in nearby Wrightsville Beach has a fully enclosed, metal dry-slip structure with four levels. Though it is only insurance rated for 100-mile-per-hour winds, the building has survived several hurricanes. As it is only about 50 yards from an ocean-facing bay, storm surge is the marina's biggest worry, so boats on the lowest level are stripped of equipment and canvas and tied down securely. Boats on the upper levels are left as is, relying on their weight and their height above a potential storm surge for safety.

Atlantic Marine

Atlantic Marine (www.atlanticmarine sales.com/services.htm), also in Wrightsville Beach, is another four-level dry-slip storage facility that is also a new-boat dealership. The building is insurance rated to 125 miles per hour, but it is an open structure like Inlet Watch's. Storm surge is also this marina's chief concern. To minimize damage, Atlantic Marine moves all client boats less than 3,000 pounds to the first level, strips them of

Dry-stack storage is not always a safe storage option. Ask your marina about the wind rating of their racks before deciding to leave your boat there or move it elsewhere. (Courtesy FEMA)

canvas and other vulnerable items, and straps them to their mounts. Like MarineMax, Atlantic Marine counts on height and weight to provide protection to boats on the upper levels. But it's interesting to note that Atlantic Marine moves its new-boat inventory inland to a service warehouse when a major storm threatens.

All three of these dry-slip storage facilities have suffered only minimal structural damage from hurricanes, but all have lost boats due to storm surge and had others damaged by flying debris. Because of the vulnerable nature of dry-stack storage, they all stress the importance of good boatowner's insurance.

Small-Boat Storage on Land

While larger boats are often safer in the water, smaller ones should almost always be removed from the water prior to an approaching storm. Dinghies, open skiffs, and other small boats that can swamp easily should be stored on land.

Having a trailer gives you options that a nontrailerable boatowner doesn't have. Probably the best place for the boat on a trailer is at your home or other property well inland, elevated above any area of potential flooding. You have greater control over this environment than any other—there are no nearby boats whose owners' carelessness will endanger yours. You can clear the area of loose material that could become airborne debris.

BOAT SURVIVAL ON A RACK

Michael Smith keeps a Four Winns 21-foot cruiser in an upper-level dry slip at Inlet Watch Yacht Club, in Wilmington, North Carolina, where he recently experienced preparing for a hurricane first-hand.

When a hurricane warning was issued, he had the boat taken off the rack and placed in the work area, where he stripped all canvas, including the boat cover, removed the seat cushions, and taped a strip of 6-mil polyethylene over the instrument panel. He also taped over all vents and hatches and removed the depth finder, then had the boat put back in its storage spot. Since there was no safe way for owners or even yard personnel to get to the upper levels to tie boats down to the structure, Michael counted on his boat's 4,400 pounds to hold it in place. Having done all he could do, he went home to wait.

The hurricane winds were not severe, but the rain was torrential. After the storm, when Michael returned to the boat, he found no damage. He did, however, have to spend a full day cleaning debris out of the boat. Leaves, tree limbs, plastic cups, dirt, and sand were strewn everywhere. On the plus side, there was no water in the boat, since the scuppers and cockpit drains did their jobs properly.

Michael is debating the merits of putting grommets in his boat cover and tying it down securely for the next storm. On the one hand, it might save him the trouble of a full day of cleanup. On the other, even with extra grommets, the wind might still rip off and destroy the cover, entailing the cost of replacement and still leaving him with the cleanup work. Or the cover, by adding windage, could increase the danger of the boat blowing off the rack.

Like everyone who faces the threat of a severe storm, Mike is learning from experience what works best for his boat and his storage situation.

Boats that are small enough can be garaged—although that may leave your car exposed, so take your pick. Otherwise, find a place in the yard that is not under trees, and that will afford the best protection from falling branches and the wind. It won't hurt to face the bow into the expected wind direction. If left on the trailer, the boat should be strapped down securely. Really small boats can be removed from the trailer and placed right on the ground. You can either fill them with water for additional weight, or turn them upside down and tie them down to stakes driven into the ground.

Davits and Lifts

Dinghies should never be left to swing on a larger boat's davits (and certainly shouldn't be left in the water on a painter!). Remove them to safe storage, or strap them upside-down on deck.

Backyard or seawall lifts are not a safe option. Boats on lifts are very exposed to high winds and damage from flying debris, and even a moderate storm surge of 10 feet will probably exceed the maximum height your boat can be raised on the lift. Even a heavy rain could cause serious problems: should your cockpit drains and scuppers become clogged with debris, the boat could fill with water, and bring the lift and boat crashing down together.

This boat is not tied down to the lift. A 4-foot surge would lift it right off the cradle and bring it down on the pilings.

8

Preparations at Slips and Docks and in Canals

Good protection in a slip, at a dock, or in a canal depends on the proper arrangement of many components. In all cases, you need to have good-quality hardware, be diligent in your maintenance, and prepare for the worst.

SLIPS AND DOCKS

Many of us don't have the choice of anchoring out and must keep our boat in a slip or at a dock, so choosing a good marina is essential. Find out how various marinas

Boats in slips should be tied with many long lines. Notice the double lines leading to the pilings, so the boat doesn't rely on the dock cleat lines to hold it in place.

came through past storms, and examine the protection their geographic situations provide from the most likely storm impacts. Look also for good engineering: docks, bulkheads, breakwaters, and buildings that are well designed, well built, and well maintained. Then there are the dock lines, the cleats and chocks on your boat, cleats on the dock itself, chafing gear, and possibly fenders. For best results, all of them must be of good quality and properly employed.

Boat Hardware

Cleats on and around boats are designed for daily use and are not really meant to handle the stress and strain of a major storm. On most manufactured boats, particu-

Properly sized cleats will hold two lines of adequate diameter for storm duty.

Although this dock cleat is through-bolted to the dock, the backing plate is merely nailed to the deck board. Strain on the cleat will certainly split the backing plate, rendering the cleat useless.

larly sailboats, they are undersized and poorly backed, and often represent a weak link in the chain of storm survivability. The larger the cleat, the better. Small cleats may work perfectly under regular conditions, but they will pinch or constrict oversized storm lines that have been substituted for normal dock lines, which will abrade the line rapidly. If you have substituted larger-diameter storm lines, use no more than two lines per cleat; any more will overload it.

After a storm, it is not unusual to find your lines intact but the cleats pulled out of the deck or dock. Even if they're through-bolted to the decking (often they're not; I've seen cleats simply nailed down!), backing plates may be absent. In either case, the decking itself is almost certainly just nailed to the stringers. If you have no choice but to use a dock cleat, be sure it is through-bolted with a backing plate.

Check the backing plate to be sure it is in good condition. Aluminum or fiberglass plates that are larger than the cleat's footprint are the best. Plywood is not as strong but, if it is in good condition, will normally be adequate. Crawl under the deck or poke a flashlight into the locker to see the backing plate.

On older boats, plywood or hardwood plates may have rotted from the constant moisture in these dark, enclosed areas. If you find anything suspicious, replace it with a larger backing plate appropriate to your boat and to the cleat in question. And as long as you're replacing it, you might as well get rid of the wood and use something more durable.

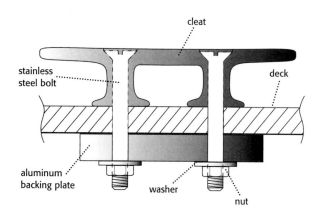

Cleats must have proper backing plates and amply sized washers, bolts, and nuts.

It's best to tie your boat to pilings; if possible, avoid tying it to cleats attached to floating docks or piers—if the dock goes, so does your boat! Unfortunately, not every slip is well equipped with multiple pilings at ideal angles for tying off, and you may have no choice but to rely on dock cleats. If you're unhappy with the cleating in your slip, see if you can get the marina to upgrade it, or get permission to do it yourself.

Be wary of cleats fastened to pilings. They're often merely lag-bolted into the wood, rather than through-bolted, and they're almost always mounted in the wrong direction: vertical, not horizontal. It's usually better to pass your dock line around the piling itself rather than tying off to a piling-mounted cleat.

This cleat is through-bolted to a fiberglass backing plate into the dock boards and should hold up. However, the cleat is only as good as the dock board.

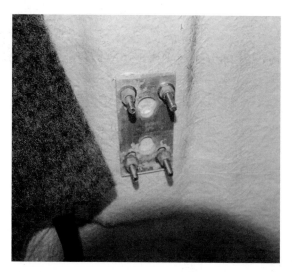

This aluminum backing plate will provide adequate support for a fairly small deck cleat.

The line leading to the dock cleat (lower right) leaves the cleat at a 90-degree angle. This puts too much strain on the cleat backing. (The line upper left is the bitter end.)

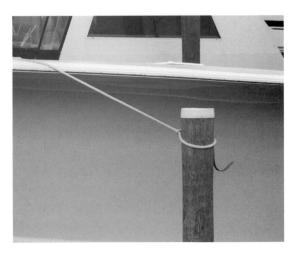

This line, which is merely looped over the piling, can be considered worthless. The bitter end should be turned around the piling three times and tied off with a few half hitches.

If your boat is underequipped at its critical tying-off points, consider upgrading all around. Though it may seem like an extravagance to replace all your backing plates, cleats, and chocks, it's actually a prudent move that can ultimately save your boat from damage and/or destruction.

Lines should lead from the cleat at a sharp angle, not perpendicular to it. Most manufacturers are aware of this and mount cleats to the deck at the proper angle for normal use. But for a good tie-off arrangement prior to a storm, lines may lead in unusual directions to reach a piling on an adjacent dock or to set an anchor at a wide angle off the bow. In most cases, try to lead the line away from the cleat at something closer to a 30-degree angle than a 90-degree angle. Again, the use of proper backing plates will strengthen the connection.

Much of what has been said for upgrading cleats applies to chocks, fairleads, and blocks. The same oversized storm line will have to pass through a chock or fairlead, which, if not upgraded to match the size of the new cleat, will simply continue the chafe and pinching problem.

One more piece of boat hardware deserves mention here: the bow pulpit.

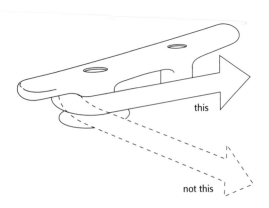

Cleats resist pull better when lines are led at shallow angles. Choose your tie-off points accordingly.

Although pulpits should never be used for tying off (they are not robust enough), they can nevertheless seriously affect the security of your tie-off arrangements. With the violent motion that a boat may experience in a slip or on a mooring during a storm, bow pulpits may come into contact with docking or mooring lines that would normally be several feet away from them. Any sharp edges on the pulpit can quickly chafe through the lines. Before the storm season begins, inspect the undersides of the pulpit tubing for rough spots or sharp edges at the welds and joints. If you find any, have them ground smooth (and replated if necessary) before the storm season begins.

Too many lines through a single chock present a serious chafing risk.

Lines

A few generalizations can be made about lines. One is that the more you use, the better your results will probably be. Another is that storm lines should be longer and larger than your normal lines, but within the limits of what your hardware can accommodate. They should be placed appropriately, protected from chafe, and relatively new.

Line degrades significantly when it is exposed to ultraviolet light for several seasons, losing much of its chafe resistance as well as tensile strength. When you consider the cost of a lost boat compared to the cost of new docking lines, it just doesn't make sense to trust old lines, even if they show no signs of wear.

Use the maximum-size line possible within the capacity of your chocks and cleats. Three-strand nylon is generally recommended over braided line for storm conditions due to its excellent combination of chafe resistance, elasticity, and breaking strength. Some people think that braided nylon and single-braid Dacron are acceptable alternatives to three-strand nylon. I believe that single-braid Dacron does not have enough stretch, while double-braided

The braided line above is so badly chafed that it will break under strain.

Recommended Sizes for Storm Dock Lines	
BOAT LENGTH (FEET)	MINIMUM LINE (THREE-STRAND LAID NYLON) DIAMETER (INCHES)
< 30	½
30–40	⅝
> 40	¾ to 1

nylon is too susceptible to abrasion for storm conditions. Some suggested storm line sizes are shown in the table.

Chafe Protection

The sustained tugging and pulling of docking lines and anchor rodes against chocks, cleats, pilings, gunwales, and pulpits during a storm can cut through even a 1-inch line in no time. Your boat and the dock it's tied to will move in three dimensions relative to one another: up and down, fore and aft, and side to side. Try to imag-

This line has no chafe protection and is showing signs of wear where it rubs on the rail.

The top line, already compromised by chafe, will develop another problem where the lines rub against each other. There is no reason they should be crossed.

The hose is sewn to the line for proper chafe protection, but the loop end of the line is not drawn through the cleat for a good connection.

There are several problems here: the line is not drawn through the cleat properly, and the protective hose has come loose, allowing heavy chafing to occur.

ine where chafing will occur with each of your lines at each direction of movement, then protect the line at every possible chafe point—wherever the line rubs, or *may* rub, against something else.

Use effective chafe protection. Duct tape, towels, and rags may look okay, but they will not last long. Plastic garden hose is a favorite for chafe protection because it is inexpensive and works well—if it's used correctly. (Rubber hose is somewhat less effective because it tends to be "grippier.")

Don't just slide a foot-long section of garden hose onto the line and jam it under a cleat. It will work loose and be no use at all. Instead, buy a length of plastic

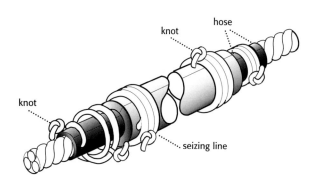

Two layers of chafe protection are better than one if the chocks and cleats are big enough to accommodate them. Use two hose sizes, drill them, and bind them to the anchor line with heavy seizing line.

garden hose, cut it into appropriate lengths and slide it over the line to the chosen location. Drill holes in both ends of each piece and, with waxed thread or nylon string, secure each end of the hose at the proper location with rolling hitches.

Splitting the hose lengthwise makes it easier to install, but it is less effective than running an uncut piece of hose onto the line from the bitter end. To be absolutely sure that chafe will not be your downfall, and if your chock and cleat are big enough, use two pieces of plastic hose. The second one should be large enough to slide over the first.

Remember, however, that most big storms occur at the end of the boating season. Months of chafing may have already weakened the line. So before you add chafe protection, inspect the line and replace it if it is worn or old.

How to Arrange Dock Lines

You can't have too many dock lines holding your boat in place, but no number will suffice if they aren't arranged properly. The number-one rule is that lines should be as long as possible and taut. In areas where there are large tidal changes, lines should be taut but also long enough to take into consideration the extra height of tide and storm surge.

Bow lines, long dock lines that run from the bow cleat through a chock to a piling well forward of the boat's bow, keep the boat from moving aft. Stern lines, long lines that run from one of the boat's stern cleats through a chock to a piling well abaft the stern, keep it from moving forward. Place the lines at the mid-tide level on the piling. If you're tying up the boat at high or low tide, try to make the lines extra tight to minimize slack at mid-tide. It's much better, however, to tie off at the time of mid-tide.

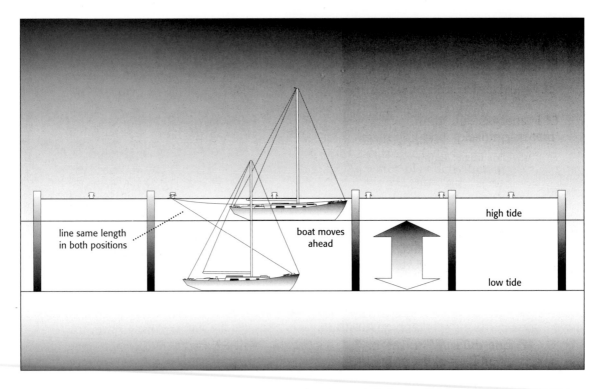

When tying up at either low or high tide, you must account for additional slackening or tightening of the lines when the tide changes. Using the longest lines possible will help.

Breast lines are short lines that lead at right angles (or nearly so) from the bow and/or stern to the dock. They keep the boat from drifting too far from the dock and can be also used to pull the boat closer to the dock for boarding.

Spring lines, like the bow and stern lines, keep the boat from moving forward or back, and because they are quite long they are particularly useful when a big tide or storm surge is expected. It's not unusual to use up to four spring lines, as follows:

- **Forward spring line:** runs from at or near the bow forward to a piling (but not as far forward as the bow line).

- **After bow spring line:** runs from the same bow location back to a piling located roughly amidships.

- **Forward quarter spring line:** runs from the stern forward to a piling located roughly amidships.

- **After quarter spring line:** runs from the stern back to a piling near where the stern line is tied down.

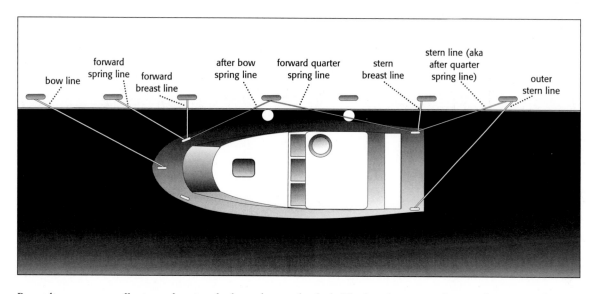

Breast lines are most effective at keeping the boat close to the dock. The bow line, spring lines, and outer stern line are most effective for preventing fore and aft movement.

If you have the good fortune to be in a slip with multiple pilings on both sides, you can use all these lines on both sides to keep your boat centered. If you're at a dock and you don't have enough pilings to accommodate the lines needed to keep your boat away from the dock, run anchor lines out to deeply imbedded anchors, one at the bow and one at the stern.

If you're expecting a big storm surge, cross two extra-long spring lines: one from the bow to the dock beyond the stern; the other from the stern to the dock forward of the bow (see illustration below and top and bottom left photos next page).

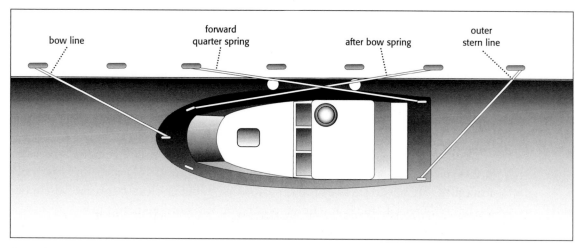

Crossed spring lines—as long as possible—are used when a significant tidal change or storm surge is expected.

Crossed spring lines—doubled, for good effect!

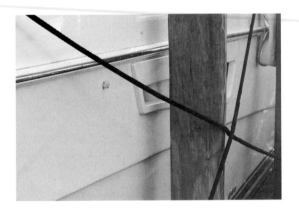

The wrong way to cross spring lines. Chafe from the piling will cut through the lines in short order.

Stripped for the storm, this boat is well tied off in an amply sized slip with double lines leading forward and numerous lines aft. Tying off to the pilings instead of the dock cleats would be an improvement.

To the extent that your hardware can accommodate it, use double dock lines. Even if you've bought new dock lines, you might as well use the old ones for a bit more insurance. Try not to tie both lines to the same piling or cleat, but spread them out so that if there is a failure at a tie-up point, you will not lose both lines.

Lines should be as long as possible—at the very least, as long as your boat—and taut. Long lines will stretch, not snap, and will let the boat ride up with the surge.

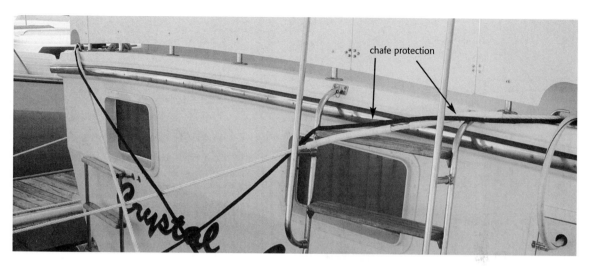

Double stern crossing lines. Note that the chafe protection that was not sewn to the line has slipped and is no longer protecting one of the docking lines from chafe against the stern ladder.

Short lines will stretch only a little before they snap. (Assuming nylon rope with 30 percent elongation, a 20-foot bow line will stretch 6 feet before breaking, while a 5-foot line will break after stretching only 1½ feet.) Use spring lines to hold the boat in the center of a slip and away from the pilings or dock. You can never use too many lines, so pile them on. Your resulting spiderweb will let your boat rise on the surge, be pummeled by the wind, and yet stay in the exact place you put it.

The photograph below right shows a clever arrangement for tying up to a piling. There is a 4- to 6-foot-long steel rod through-bolted to the piling. A shackle, fastened

This boat is being held off the dock by very long lines tied to pilings in the next slip.

This steel rod has been through-bolted to the piling, allowing the docking lines shackled to the rod to rise at least 5 feet with high water.

Commercial rubber or vinyl snubbers are available to take up some of the shock loading on docking lines.

to the end of the docking line, is connected to the steel rod and will ride up and down with changes in water level. This somewhat mitigates the need for stretch on this particular line, but its use is pretty much confined to bow and stern lines, not to springs, which still need to be long, tight, and stretchy.

When a dock line is rapidly forced to the end of its stretch limits, it hardens, and the boat will receive quite a jerk (called shock loading), even though the line will bear a lot of additional strain before breaking. This jerk can be uncomfortable for people on the boat in the slip, so many boaters use commercial rubber or plastic snubbers that absorb the shock during the dock line's last few inches of stretch. I do not recommend these for use in storm preparations, however. In my experience, they are not strong enough for tough jobs, and they deteriorate rapidly in the salt/sun environment. If one breaks during a storm, the result is slack in the line—a far worse situation than the one the snubber was meant to mitigate.

Tying Off

When tying a line to a piling, make at least two turns around the piling without overlapping the line and secure it with three half hitches. This configuration places almost all the strain on the two turns and not on the knots. The knots, which are normally the weakest point in a line, need only hold the turns in place and keep the line from slipping up or down. Bowlines and cinch knots are not suggested as they can pinch and chafe.

If you are using dock lines with an eye-spliced end, the eye should be on the boat's cleat, and the bitter end on the dock or piling. That way, marina personnel or emergency crews can easily adjust a chafed or compromised line at the dock or piling. They will be

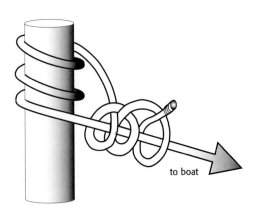

to boat

Tie off to a piling by taking at least two turns around a piling, followed by three half hitches.

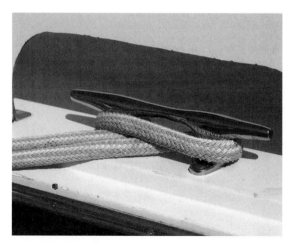

Feed the loop end of a docking line through the hole in the cleat, then flip it over the cleat ends to give a safe, strong connection.

A knot tied to make a loop and then just hung over a cleat does not give a reliable connection.

much less willing to board your boat to make a similar adjustment at your boat's cleats, even if it is safe and practical to do so.

The best way to load a cleat is to pass a well-made eye splice through its center hole and loop it over the horns (see photo left top). If you must make a loop by knotting a line, make sure the knot is far enough away from the cleat to prevent undue abrasion.

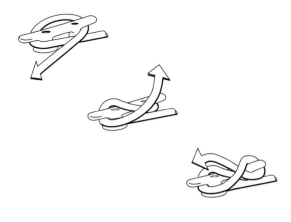

Another cleat tie-off is the basic figure-eight. Lead the line around the base of the cleat, over and under one end, then loop it over the other end and pull it tight. Simple, quick, and effective.

Five docking lines and a fender attached to one midship cleat is a classic example of overloading.

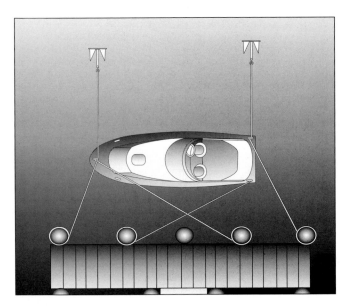

When tying up alongside a dock, position the boat as far off the dock as possible, with lines to pilings or anchors to keep it off.

Tie no more than two lines to any cleat, as more will inevitably cause jamming and chafe. If the boat has trailer connections, use them as additional tie-off points. Use as many lines and tie-off points as possible. The docking line arrangement may look like a spiderweb when you are done, but this isn't a beauty contest.

Positioning the Boat

To reduce windage and battering from waves, point the bow toward the expected storm direction or open water. A boat with its broad side exposed to the full force of the wind will roll and put additional strain on the dock lines.

If you're in a slip, you want to be centered side-to-side, with your bow or stern as far as possible from the dock without interfering with the fairway and so you can still get aboard. If you are laid up sideways against a dock, do whatever you can to position the boat as far from the dock as possible. If you have a choice, tie up on the expected lee side of the dock, so that wind and waves will push your boat away from the dock, not force your boat against it. If possible, run lines to trees or distant pilings to help hold the boat off the dock. If not, use at least two anchors—one each from the bow and stern. Use your dinghy to take them out as far as practical, making sure they're set securely. Run bow and stern lines as long as possible, with the stern line secured on the cleat on the side of boat away from the dock, and long, crossed springs.

If the boat will be stern-to the dock, run dual bow lines to pilings or well-embedded anchors. Use the longest lines possible. Spring lines should be shorter and connected to pilings on

"Why didn't he tie to the pilings?"

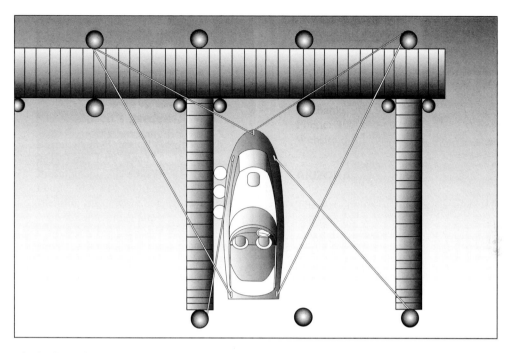

The fenders will not protect this boat, which is too close to the dock. If the other slip is vacant, the owner should position the boat in the middle of the space.

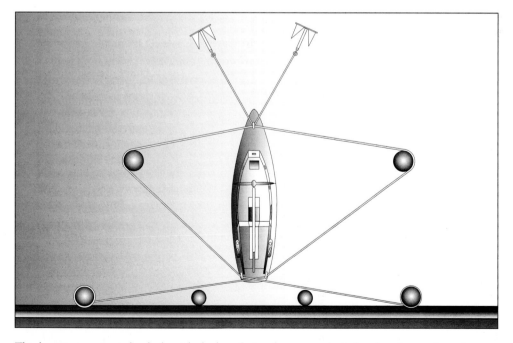

This boat is stern-to at the dock, with the bow facing the expected wind and anchors to keep the boat off. Use crossed stern lines, as long as possible, and shorter spring lines tied to pilings.

In the rush to prepare for the approaching storm, the owner of this boat did not have time to strip the mizzen sail and the bimini canvas. Wrapping them tightly is always a poor second choice. I would have liked to see crossed stern lines and crossed spring lines added as well as bow lines to the pilings.

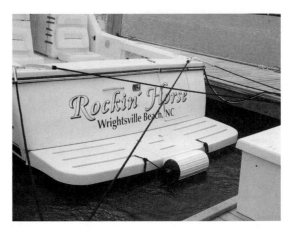

Crossed stern lines along with the normal stern lines will keep the boat dead center in the slip. Prior to a storm, it would be good to remove the shore-power cable as the power will probably go out anyway.

either side of the boat. Stern lines may be crossed, which will facilitate the use of slightly longer lines.

Fenders

Most boatowners who keep their boat in a slip or at a dock use a few fenders to keep the topsides from rubbing up and down on pilings or the dock itself. Under normal conditions, cylindrical fenders do a good job of protecting a boat from the effects of boat wakes, waves, and tidal changes. But when a storm is violently pushing boat and dock around, most cylindrical fenders will compress so much as to be ineffective. Ball-type fenders are gaining in popularity as they seem to be tougher and more effective, but because they have no tie-offs on the bottom, they're difficult, if not impossible, to keep properly positioned.

Many experts advise putting out as many fenders as possible as part of your storm preparations, but experience has shown that they seldom do much good. Properly arranged dock lines will keep your boat off the dock and the pilings; fenders won't cut it.

However, fenders may, in fact, provide a false sense of security that keeps some owners from taking more effective measures. That won't happen to you, of course, so *after* you've properly secured your boat with docking lines, go ahead and use fenders—as many as you have—on the gunwale facing *away* from the dock; i.e., the side exposed to possible hits from other boats. They probably won't do much good, but they certainly won't hurt.

Too often, fenders are crushed by extreme loads pressing the hull against the dock. If they are flat, they provide little protection to the boat's hull.

Ball fenders can take a tremendous load, even from a large boat, and still maintain their shape, but they're hard to keep in place.

The same holds true for fender boards. While they do provide a wider area of coverage than individual fenders, and tend to prevent the fenders from rolling out of the way, they still provide, at best, minimal protection if a boat is being battered against the edge of a dock by storm-driven waves. In fact, they might even do more harm than good if they are crushed against the boat's topsides, possibly scratching or puncturing the hull.

CANALS, WATERWAYS, AND CREEKS

Preparations to ride out a storm in a canal, creek, or other narrow waterway are similar to marina preparations in many respects. In both venues, the boat is tied off to fixed objects, although in the case of canals and creeks, those objects are farther from the boat and the lines are longer. Unlike preparations for anchoring and mooring, where the boat is allowed to swing in a wide circle to face the wind, the objective in canal and creek preparation is to hold the boat in a fixed position.

As discussed in Chapter 7, you should move your boat to the middle of the canal and tie off to both sides of the waterway as soon as possible. Two days is usually enough time to make good preparations and still provide a reasonable window of opportunity for anyone with a boat landward of you to evacuate. You'll have to weigh the relative threats of wind and current and, if they will be opposed to each other, face the bow toward the worst of the expected threats.

With a typical 100-foot-wide canal, there will be a long stretch for the lines to reach shore. But as we have seen, the longer the lines, the better. Use three-strand nylon line with at least ¾-inch diameter. I have seen too many braided dock lines badly chafed, while a three-strand nylon line right next to it showed no chafe damage at all.

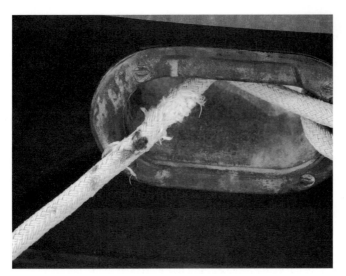

With no chafe protection, this braided line is almost worn through from wear against the chock.

Put out as many lines as possible by cross-tying to every tree, piling, mangrove, stump, or embedded anchor you can reach on both shores. If you are in a waterway that is too narrow to allow swinging at anchor but too wide to reach both sides with a multiplicity of your longest lines, you may need to use anchors to port and starboard. A dinghy comes in handy for delivering storm anchors to the perfect positions before they are dropped and set. Even if you're well tied off to both shores, add as many anchors as possible to both sides of the boat and to the expected windward direction. The arrangement will probably look strange, but we're interested in safety, not aesthetics.

Double the bow and stern lines and use single spring lines to hold the boat in place. If the wind is expected to come from the side rather than straight up or down the canal, double the lines on that side as well.

Add chafe protection at every possible chafe point. Once a line is badly chafed, its strength is reduced dramatically and cannot be counted on. During a lull in the storm, you may have an opportunity to replace a chafed or broken line, so keep at least 350 extra feet of uncut ¾-inch line handy in the garage. Don't take personal risks to do this, however.

Even if your tying-off preparations are perfect, you still may be at risk from other boats that break away from their berths and come bearing down on yours with the wind or current. There's not much you can do to protect your lines, but you can provide at least a little protection against a direct strike on your boat by placing fenders. As previously mentioned, many boatowners have found that ball fenders are tougher and more reliable than conventional cylindrical ones. For a 40-foot boat, place at least three ball fenders on each side.

Two-Boat Raft

A relatively new arrangement used to secure boats in Florida canals during the hurricanes of 2004 proved very effective and will undoubtedly become more popular. Two boats are rafted together mid-stream and tied tightly together with as many ball fenders as possible between them. There are many more boat cleats available with two boats sandwiched together, allowing for more lines to shore or to anchors. In the

2004 storms, doubled-up boats rode out the hurricanes with no problems while single boats nearby had numerous failures. It's unclear why this system worked so well—it may be that the greater mass of the two connected boats provided greater inertia to resist the short jerking motions from the multitude of smaller waves; in any case, it shows great promise.

LIGHTNING PROTECTION

Lightning presents a special danger to boatowners. It often strikes the highest object in a given area, and since boats, by their nature, float on the surface of the water, they represent very common targets. It is also attracted to metal. Sailboat masts are usually the highest object in marinas or anchorages, but even small powerboats typically have metal appendages several feet above the water's surface and are therefore at risk.

Once lightning strikes, the electrical charge will take the most direct route to ground (which in the case of a boat is the water) where the charge will dissipate. A lightning protection system provides the most direct path possible, so that the charge doesn't head off in dangerous directions—such as through the hull, through the air from one component to another, or through a person. This is no trivial risk: some 13 percent of lightning deaths occur on boats.

To protect your boat from lightning, be sure all components that conduct electricity are electrically bonded together and adequately grounded. Unbonded components may result in side flashes, as the electrical charge jumps from one component to another trying to reach a path to ground.

Boat hulls made of metal are rarely damaged by lightning. While these boats are struck as frequently as boats built from other materials (if not more so), the high conductivity of the hull provides a large, low-resistance, direct path to ground. In addition, the hull is a huge metal surface area that is in direct contact with the water, allowing rapid dissipation of the charge.

Wood and fiberglass, on the other hand, are not electrically conductive, and boats made of these materials do not provide a good path for lightning to pass through safely. If the electrical current must seek a route to ground through nonconductive material, the material itself will absorb the charge, which may well result in a fire or even outright vaporization of hull material. If you happen to be part of that path to ground . . . well, let's just say this is something to avoid. The best way to avoid injury, therefore, is to stay off your boat when a storm threatens, or get off it as quickly as possible. If you are caught on your boat when lightning is flashing all around, stay in the cabin, or low and in the center of the boat if there is no cabin, and as far away from any metal parts as possible.

But since there is a strong possibility that lightning may someday strike your boat, whether you are on it or not, you should have the best lightning protection possible. This is not a do-it-yourself project: seek out a boatyard with staff qualified to inspect your boat, determine its degree of protection, and correct any shortcomings. Have the system inspected annually, before storm season begins.

Lightning Protection Systems

A boat's lightning protection system consists of three main components: an air terminal, a main conductor, and a ground. Other parts of the system include secondary conductors and connectors and special devices to isolate sensitive electronic equipment.

The air terminal—essentially a lightning rod—should be a highly conductive material extending at least 6 inches above the top of the mast (on a sailboat) or anything else on the boat. If lightning does strike, this will ensure that it does so on your terms. Antennas and outriggers can serve as air terminals if they are of sufficient conductivity and properly connected to the main conductor.

The main conductor can be a metal mast or a length of copper cable or metal strapping specified for sufficient conductivity that runs from the air terminal to the ground.

The ground can be a metal plate attached to the surface of the hull or other exposed metal parts below the waterline. The ground should present at least 1 square foot of surface area in contact with the water, and it should be made of a noncorrosive metal like copper. In practice, this can be difficult to achieve, because large surfaces of unprotected metal can create galvanic corrosion problems. Painting the metal significantly reduces this problem by reducing its conductivity with the water, but it equally reduces the metal's functionality as a ground.

Secondary conductors should lead from every major metal component on the boat to the main conductor. (Carbon fiber, or graphite, is highly conductive. Components made from lightweight graphite composites should be treated like metal and properly bonded.) Grounding dozens of components throughout the boat with secondary conductors essentially surrounds the interior spaces with a conductive cage that protects the people and contents. Radios and electronic equipment should have lightning arrestors (i.e., surge suppressors) and lightning-protective gaps (two closely spaced electrodes that allow the charge to arc across) to protect them from electrical surges.

Lightning protection on a sailboat means diverting the lightning current into the water so that it passes around or through the boat without causing damage or injury. This involves providing a continuous, mainly vertical, conducting path from a height above any vulnerable masthead transducers all the way down to grounding conductors immersed in the water (i.e., the grounding system). Attached to the main vertical conducting path is a network of mostly horizontal conductors connected to large metal fittings and to the boat's electrical grounding system. Transient voltage surge suppressors are needed on each piece of electronics equipment, and wiring should all be twisted pair for protection of electronics.

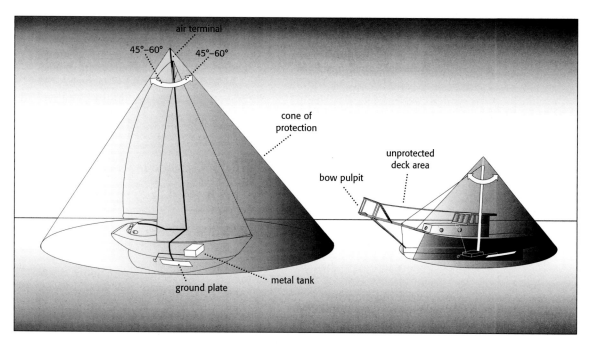

An air terminal—a properly grounded lightning rod—provides a cone of protection. (This may leave part of the deck unprotected.) All major metal components are bonded to the main conductor.

Special attention must be paid to providing a main conductor path on sailboats with masts that don't contact the keel, including small boats with readily dismountable masts and boats with masts mounted on the cabin top.

A properly protected mast or other air terminal provides a cone-shaped area of protection with its apex at the top of the terminal and its base at the water's surface. There is some dispute, however, about the length of the cone's radius and, thus, the size of the area protected. In most cases, the radius probably ranges from one to two times the height of the air terminal. The deck area of most sailboats, therefore, falls completely within the protected zone. Many powerboats, on the other hand, do not have a metal appendage tall enough to protect the entire deck area. If this is the case with your boat, you can raise the air terminal or install additional lightning protection circuits.

GROUNDING WORKS . . . TO A DEGREE

A few years ago, three couples went boating on the Severn River near Annapolis, Maryland. All were experienced, local boating people, and the boat was carefully maintained, with a professionally installed lightning protection system in place. When a thunderstorm hit unexpectedly, the women went below and the men stayed on deck, one at the wheel and the others battening down anything loose. Lightning hit the boat, and all three men were knocked out. Fortunately, no one was killed, but the men were hospitalized with various injuries. Each lost his hearing, one permanently. The women below were unhurt. Had the boat not been grounded properly, even more serious injuries or even death would almost certainly have occurred.

The National Fire Protection Association (NFPA) Lightning Protection Code also suggests the following:

- The main conductor, from the top of the mast to the ground plate, should be as straight as possible. Any bends should have a minimum radius of 8 inches.
- The entire circuit should have a minimum conductivity equivalent to #8 AWG copper conductor.
- Major metal components within 6 feet of the lightning conductor should be connected to it with #8 AWG copper or better.
- The engine should be grounded directly to the ground plate.
- Antennas and anything else that extends above the mast or presents an alternate target should be tied down or removed during a storm.
- All materials used in a lightning protection system should be corrosion resistant.
- The "water ground" may be any sufficiently noncorrosive metal (e.g., copper, Monel, or bronze) below the waterline, with at least 1 square foot of exposed surface area. Propellers, rudders, skegs, or metal hulls can be used, or a special grounding plate may be installed for the purpose.
- On sailboats, the entire rig (including all spars, shrouds, stays, sail tracks, etc.) should be bonded and grounded.

Lightning protection systems don't prevent lightning strikes. They may, in fact, increase the probability of the boat being struck by intentionally poking a lightning rod into the sky. The main purpose of lightning protection is to reduce the damage to the boat and the possibility of injuries or death from a lightning strike. You can't make a boat lightning *proof*; you can, however, *protect* it to a significant degree.

Preparations on Moorings and at Anchor

9

There is no perfect solution to the problem of where to locate a boat for weathering a storm. Each location has its advantages and disadvantages. Anchoring and mooring are no exceptions.

The greatest advantage of anchoring and mooring your boat is that it will be better able to handle storm surge and changes in wind direction. No matter how high the surge, an anchored or moored boat will ride it, provided it has sufficient scope. And regardless of the wind's direction, the boat will always face into it, presenting the least possible windage and smallest possible target for battering waves. An additional advantage of anchoring is the possibility of finding a refuge away from other boats, eliminating the danger of boats or docks slamming into yours.

On the other hand, the disadvantages are quite obvious. Even when you have multiple anchors out, the rodes will be fewer in number than the many dock lines you would use in a slip. At the dock, if one or two dock lines part, there are plenty more to do the job. But if you lose an anchor line, the one or two remaining rodes are put under acute strain. Compounding this problem is the almost constant tug and release on the rode, which can cause rapid chafing even if you are using the best antichafe protection.

These boats are anchored too close. After a collision with the powerboat, the sailboat may already be dragging toward the soft shore.

And, of course, there is the possibility that an anchor can drag if it is not set deep enough in a good holding bottom, aligned correctly, and of sufficient size and type.

Note: Much of what applies to slip and dock storage, especially in regard to chafe protection and proper sizing and installation of cleats, applies equally to anchoring and mooring. Refer to the previous chapter for this important information.

PERMANENT MOORINGS

Permanent moorings are assembled from a number of parts: a well-set anchor, a chain from the anchor to a buoy, and a pendant from the buoy to a pickup float.

Although successful moorings have many configurations, one reliable system consists of a heavy chain one and a half times longer than the depth of the water at high tide fastened by a shackle to the anchor. At the other end is a swivel/shackle combination attaching a lighter-weight chain long enough to reach from the bottom to the mooring buoy at high tide. This arrangement keeps most of the chain on the bottom, with a long catenary (sag or curve in the chain) that puts the least amount of strain on the buried anchor.

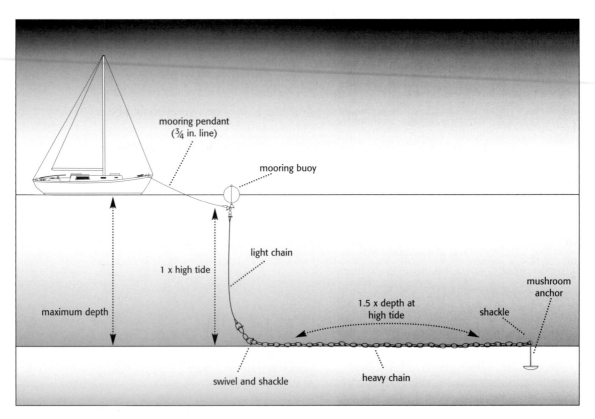

This is a reliable, all-chain mooring arrangement for normal conditions. For storm conditions, the rode should be extended with a length of heavy nylon line for greater scope.

Mooring anchors are available in various price ranges. Most clubs and marinas use heavy mushroom anchors that, in time, bury themselves deep in the bottom. Helical mooring anchors, such as those from Helix Mooring Systems (www.helixmooringsys tems.com), that screw into the bottom of the harbor are reportedly more effective. But they are expensive and few anchorages use them since mushrooms give adequate performance under most circumstances.

At the low end of the cost-and-effectiveness spectrum are large concrete blocks. These do not bury themselves in the bottom but rely on deadweight to stay put. Before specifying or accepting a mooring with a concrete or other deadweight anchor, consider the following:

1. A deadweight anchor weighs approximately 50% less in the water than it does on land, so its holding power will be reduced. For example, a 5,000-pound concrete anchor will provide only 2,500 pounds of holding power.
2. A mooring failure does not require the deadweight to be lifted clear of the bottom—only dragged.

Another worthwhile mooring arrangement consists of three lightweight anchors, such as the Danforth or Fortress type (but as heavy as you can handle), working as a team. A short rode from each anchor leads to a bridle at a central point, where they are connected with shackles and a swivel to the main rode. The swivel should be as large as possible.

This system has multiple advantages: There are always at least two anchors to windward of the boat, regardless of the direction of the wind. The boat swings through a smaller arc than it would on a conventional mooring, which allows mooring fields to be more densely populated (useful in crowded anchorages where scope must be limited). And the shorter length of rode up from the bridle to the bow minimizes "tacking" of the boat at anchor. Even with its lightweight anchors, this arrangement seems to have the holding power of a heavier, conventional permanent mooring (see top illustration next page).

No matter what anchor type you use, regularly check all your permanent mooring components to be sure the tackle is sound and that the anchors remain buried upright. Mushroom anchors will do a satisfactory job if they are deeply buried straight up and down and not tilted to the side (see bottom illustration next page). To be sure, dive down to the bottom and take a look on a nice summer day, or hire a diver to do it for you.

Before a big storm, consider adding a piece of heavy nylon line between the mooring buoy and the upper end of the chain to act as a shock absorber. The nylon line should be equivalent to about 10 percent of the length of the main chain rode and

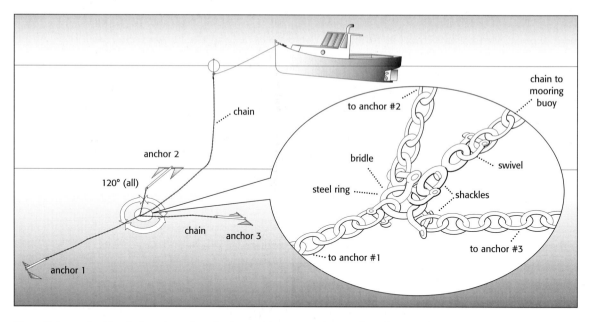

Three lightweight, Danforth-style anchors leading to a common chain rode make a good mooring setup for crowded anchorages.

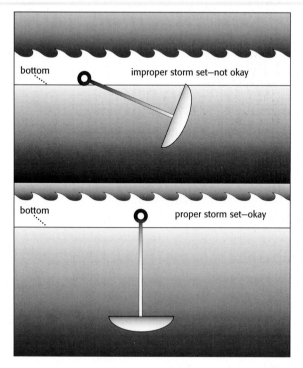

Mushroom anchors must be buried vertically to remain effective.

should, of course, be properly eye-spliced with thimbles and fastened to the chain and the buoy with shackles and swivels. An even better approach is to create a sagging loop (catenary) of approximately 15 feet of chain by tying a 10-foot length of strong nylon line above and below the sagging chain. The nylon line will absorb the shock of the jerking that will occur as the boat dances around during the storm, but if the nylon line parts, the chain will still hold.

Moorings may rely on a scope of as little as 2.5:1 for normal conditions, but it's important to add as much additional scope as possible in preparation for a storm. A ratio of 10:1 is considered the minimum acceptable, although this can be difficult to arrange in many mooring fields.

Some yacht clubs and marinas have storm plans that include a thinning out procedure (pulling some boats out of the water or requiring some of them to relocate) to enable the remaining boats to let out more scope without endangering any neighboring boats. During a storm, there should be at least one and one half times the total scope plus the boat's length between each boat in the mooring field. More, if feasible, cannot hurt.

Some marinas also require moored boats to add a second pendant early in the season to improve their chances of survival in strong storms. A second ¾-inch nylon pendant between the mooring chain shackle and the bow is sufficient for most boats.

Remember, always place heavy-duty chafe protection at the chocks and cleats.

ANCHORING

While a well-engineered and well-maintained mooring will hold your boat better than any portable anchor your boat can carry, there are times and situations where anchoring is the preferable option—if not the only one. By carefully tracking storm warnings, you may have determined that your regular mooring is dangerously exposed to the anticipated direction of the storm's winds. Or you may feel that hazards within the harbor to windward of you—poorly secured boats or poorly maintained docks, for example—put your boat at undue risk, regardless of how well you might prepare your own mooring. And, of course, if you're not in your home port, and you can't find an open mooring or slip at a local marina, you may have no choice but to anchor out. Fortunately, there are a number of anchoring arrangements that have proven successful in extreme storm conditions.

Anchor Selection

Choosing an anchor for your boat is almost as personal a decision as your choice of the boat itself. There are numerous designs and weights, ranging from sporty, light-weight types used as "lunchhooks" to heavy-duty models for storm purposes. But what you need in a storm anchor is not just the best holding-power-to-weight ratio, it's the greatest holding power—period.

Having said that so definitively, I'll immediately qualify it by adding: you need the greatest holding power *for the bottom conditions*. If you know exactly where you'll weather a storm, you should buy the anchor that holds best in that type of bottom. If you might be in the midst of a cruise when a storm approaches, you should choose the anchor (or anchors) that provides the best holding power across a variety of bottoms. But don't be concerned about overkill when choosing a storm anchor. Get the biggest and heaviest anchor(s) you and your boat can handle.

Since the anchor must be suited to the bottom, you can approach anchor selection and storm site selection from two different directions. You can find a hurricane hole with the type of bottom best suited to your anchors, or you can buy the most appropriate anchors for the anchorage you have chosen.

Forged-metal anchors are generally stronger than cast-metal types. Most light-weight anchors are not good at resetting themselves and don't set well in grass. Some,

A good view of the pivoting blade of a CQR anchor.

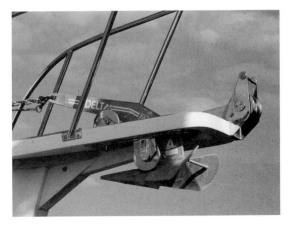

The Delta anchor with its high-tensile plow.

however, such as the heaviest Fortress anchors, have extremely high holding power for their weight and may be helpful in a multiple anchoring setup.

The small-boat anchors that seem to work best for almost all boaters in the vast majority of situations fall into two categories. The first is the plow anchor, which has a single plow-like fluke that buries deep. The second is known variously as the Danforth type, lightweight, or double fluke, and is probably familiar to every boatowner.

Plow anchors work well in sand or mud but are not as efficient in grass or rock. They come in both pivoting and nonpivoting varieties. Both types reset quite well and resist fouling their rodes when the direction of pull is changed. The CQR anchor is an example of a pivoting type, with a hinge at the end of the shank. The Delta anchor looks similar to the CQR, but it is a nonpivoting, or one-piece, anchor. This seems to give it better holding power.

The Bruce anchor with its unique three-pronged plow.

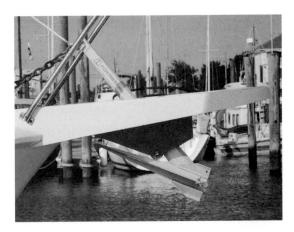

The lightweight Fortress anchor has adjustable flukes that are hinged for easy penetration.

Although it looks quite different, the Bruce anchor is considered to be a plow anchor variant. It has no moving parts and sets easily in mud, sand, coral, and rock. It can hit the bottom at any angle, and will right itself and dig in immediately. Once set, it holds very well even when there is a wide change in the direction of pull, but it is easily broken out when pulling it up.

In the lightweight category, the Danforth and Fortress pivoting fluke anchors are quite popular. A large Fortress anchor is a good alternative choice to a Danforth since it has adjustable flukes whose angle can be set to maximize their ability to dig into and hold in various bottoms.

Many other designs, including the Spade, Océane, and Bulwagga exist, and each has its proponents, benefits, and liabilities. The traditional yachtsman style (aka a stock or kedge anchor) penetrates well through heavy weed and grass, but it doesn't ride well in bow chocks or rollers and can easily foul its rode on the exposed fluke, so few boaters use it.

Appropriate sizes and weights of anchors vary considerably with the design, bottom conditions, manufacturer's test assumptions, and unfortunately, marketing tactics. Some manufacturers provide a single recommendation based on a boat's length overall, while others distinguish between power and sail, break down the length categories into additional classes by weight, and provide different recommendations for working anchors and storm conditions (the definitions of which may vary between manufacturers). If the manufacturer does not make such distinctions, it's usually prudent to assume that the given recommendation is for "working" or general conditions, and to select an anchor at least one size larger for storm conditions—generally, but not universally, considered to be Force 9 and above (winds of 41 knots and higher). Likewise, if the manufacturer's recommendations don't distinguish between sail and power, go up at least one (more) size to accommodate the greater windage of powerboats. As a general rule, for hurricanes and other major storms, always use the biggest anchors you can handle and your boat can accommodate.

The table next page lists recommended weights for some popular anchors. Some of the storm anchor recommendations come directly from the manufacturers, while others are derived from the manufacturers' working anchor recommendations using the best available information.

My personal choice for storm use in most situations is the largest, heaviest Fortress anchor I can handle. But since no two anchoring situations are the same, you should acquire an inventory of anchors suitable to your boat and to every storm situation you might encounter. Talk to your neighbors in the marina; talk to marina management; talk to local outfitters. Local information is often invaluable to a newcomer.

But don't expect the anchor to do all the work. Anchors function within a context of many variables, including a boat's weight and windage; the type, size, and condition of the rode and its associated hardware; the amount of scope paid out; and the

Suggested Anchor Sizes for Storm Conditions

BOAT LENGTH OVERALL (FEET)	ANCHOR TYPE (WEIGHT IN POUNDS)				
	BRUCE	CQR		DANFORTH (STANDARD)	
	Storm (manufacturer's data)	Working (manufacturer's data)	Storm (derived)	Working (20+ knots; manufacturer's data)	Storm (derived)
< 20	11	–	–	5	9
20–30	16.5	15	20	9	16
30–40	22	36	45	16	25
40–50	44	45	60	43	43
50–60	66	60	75	70	70

Source: Alain Poiraud

size and bedding of chocks and cleats. Each variable demands careful attention, as the failure of just one component can easily render all other arrangements ineffective.

Line, Chain, and Shackles

The most common anchor line is three-strand nylon. It stretches up to 30 percent under load, which helps absorb the huge pulls and tugs that could overload a boat's fittings and/or the ground tackle during a storm. It is also relatively lightweight and easy to handle. It is far from perfect, however. It is highly subject to chafe and can be easily abraded on rough rocks or coral.

Another option is polyester line (often identified by the trade name Dacron). It has less elasticity than nylon, so it is not recommended for the main rode, but it is more resistant to chafe than nylon. Consider using a short length of polyester line to pass through a chock, then join it to a nylon rode with a good, fail-safe attachment, such as thimbled eyes and shackles.

A heavy, all-chain rode offers significant advantages over a nylon-chain combination rode. It would take a very strong wind to lift an all-chain rode completely off the bottom—and a stronger one still before the rode loses its catenary (sag) and becomes straight enough to apply direct tension on the anchor itself. And an anchor can't possibly drag as long as there is slack in the rode. Furthermore, the angle at which the rode meets the anchor will always be shallower with a heavier rode than a lighter one, and anchors are far less likely to break loose under such conditions.

While chain lacks the elasticity that makes nylon shock absorbing, the catenary in a chain has much the same effect. Only under truly extreme conditions, when the

DELTA		FORTRESS		SPADE	SWORD
Working (manufacturer's data)	Storm (derived)	Working (manufacturer's data)	Storm (derived)	Storm (manufacturer's data)	Storm (manufacturer's data)
14	14	4	7	13	–
14	22	7	10	22	9
22	35	10	21	33	18
35	44	15/21	32	44	26
44	55	32	47	66	35

wind is so strong that the chain rode has been pulled entirely straight, does the chain lose this function. At that point, any additional wind gusts or waves may cause the anchor to break loose or severe jerks and tugs to be transmitted to the boat's hardware, but chances are that an anchor on a nylon rode would have broken loose or dragged long before that point.

Elasticity can be added to an all-chain rode by adding a snubber of three-strand nylon line. Using swivels and shackles, attach about 10 to 20 feet of three-strand nylon line to the chain at two points, which allows a length of chain about 15 percent longer to sag into the water from the points of attachment. As the boat jerks around under the action of wind and waves, most of the shock will be absorbed by the snubber, helping isolate the boat's hardware, and protecting the anchor itself from much of the jerking action that could break it out of the bottom.

Another configuration of this nylon shock absorber concept is to bypass a short length of chain at the bow. Tie one end of a 10-foot length of nylon line to a solid deck cleat and lead it

The anchor chain, which is about 6 feet off the bow, has had the tension taken off it by a double line of three-strand nylon. The nylon line runs from bow cleats to a shackle 6 feet down the anchor chain. Above the shackle, a few feet of chain hang loose while the nylon line takes up the shock load of the boat dancing in the wind.

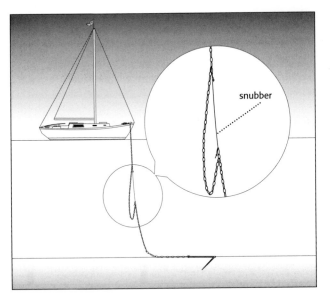

snubber

A snubber, made from a 6-foot length of nylon line, bypasses a small section of chain rode. It will help absorb shocks, thus protecting the boat's hardware and the anchor's set.

through a bow chock to a point about 10 feet down on the set anchor chain and attach the other end of the nylon line to the chain with a shackle. Feed 6 to 8 feet of chain out of the chain locker so that the chain above the attached line hangs loose.

While the weight of chain confers advantages, it also makes the rode difficult to handle, requiring a windlass for all but the strongest boatowners. Also, under normal cruising conditions the extra weight in the chain locker can create problems with trim and handling. The alternative is a combination rode (part chain, part nylon), which is probably the most popular and effective all-purpose storm rode.

Although the ratio of chain to line will vary with conditions (and a boater's preferences), a common arrangement is to attach a 6- to 10-foot length of chain to the anchor with a shackle. At the other end of this chain is second shackle, to which a full length of appropriately sized nylon line is attached with an eye splice and thimble. The chain adds a catenary to the line and will lie on the bottom, providing a good, shallow angle of pull against the anchor, and it will not chafe from rocks or coral as line would. More than 6 to 10 feet of chain is better, but overall, the combination rode is fairly lightweight and easy to retrieve and handle.

Whether you use an all-chain rode or a line/chain combination, if you use a swivel between the anchor shackle and the chain rode, use the largest one feasible as it is a weak point in the system. And be sure to use excellent chafe protection where the line rode passes through chocks, over rollers, and anywhere else it rubs.

Scope

The amount of scope, which affects the angle of pull on the rode, may be the most important factor influencing whether your anchor will hold or drag. You want a scope ratio of at least 10:1, which means your rode should be at least ten times as long as the vertical distance from the bottom to your bow chock.

Be careful to account for all aspects of that vertical distance. Start with the water depth at high tide and add the height of potential storm surge; the sum is called the maximum depth. Then add the distance from the water's surface to the bow chock for the total height. If you're using a depth sounder, don't forget to account for its depth below the surface.

Let's run through an example, using these conditions:

- Charted depth at mean high tide is 20 feet.
- The bow chock is 5 feet above the water's surface.
- A Category 2 storm with a storm surge of 6 to 8 feet is expected.

Therefore: (20 + 5 + 8) x 10 = 330 feet of scope. This is your *minimum*; more is better.

With a 10:1 scope, those few feet of chain on a line/chain rode will lie flat on the bottom, and the resulting low angle of pull will actually help dig the anchor in

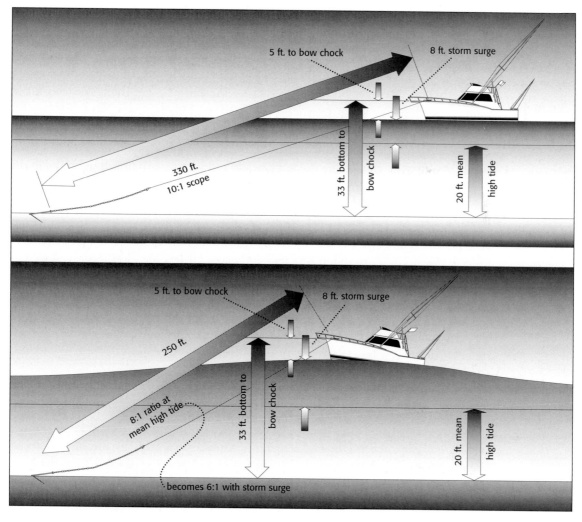

Storm surge can greatly reduce the scope of your anchor rode. Make sure you have plenty of scope—at least 10:1 on top of the projected storm surge.

deeper. This should give you some comfort. If you skimp even a little bit on the length of your rode, however, and fail to account for storm surge, your scope ratio drops rapidly. Chances are then good that the storm will jerk even the best anchor out of the bottom, and the boat will drag. Even if you should be so unfortunate—or so foolish—as to be aboard at the time, resetting a dragging anchor is almost impossible in the middle of a storm.

How do you know how much anchor rode you've paid out? You should mark your anchor line with fathom or foot markers. Sets of small plastic flags with marker numbers printed on them can be easily fastened to laid nylon line. These are available in almost every marine supply store. If you have an all-chain rode, spray-paint a dozen links or so at intervals of 30 to 50 feet, using a different color on each section. This will clearly signal the amount of chain passing through the windlass even on a stormy afternoon.

Trip Lines

Using trip lines is a fairly common practice for boats anchoring in rocky or weedy bottoms. Anchors often get hung up, and a trip line can help get them out. You might want to use this trick for storm anchoring, even in sandy bottoms, since you're going to such lengths to make sure the anchor is embedded as deeply and firmly as possible.

To make a trip line, tie a line to the anchor's crown and lead it up to a small buoy. When you're ready to retrieve the anchor, just pull on the trip line. This will pull the anchor backward, making it simple to break it out.

Rollers

A well-found bow roller is preferable to a stationary chock for storm anchoring. A roller is much kinder to nylon line and will cause far less abrasion (but even so, you still need to install chafing gear). And because a roller is usually located on a boat's centerline, it helps keep the bow dead to the wind. Most chocks, which are set back a small distance along the gunwales, may allow the boat to tack back and forth through the wind, putting additional strain on the ground tackle. Make sure the roller hardware is robust; some are not engineered for hard use.

STORM ANCHORING TECHNIQUES

If you've found an ideal hurricane hole, with a heavily forested, windward shore, you can tie your bow off to some solid tree trunks. Let the boat fall back as far as possible on the bow line (or preferably, lines), then make two trips in the dinghy to set anchors off the boat's stern, as widely separated and as far as possible from the boat. If you can, dive to the bottom to make sure the anchors are dug in well. If diving isn't possible, test the set by pulling on the lines as hard as you can.

If you cannot tie off to trees on shore, use three storm anchors set on separate rodes 120 degrees apart. In this arrangement, there is always at least one anchor—and

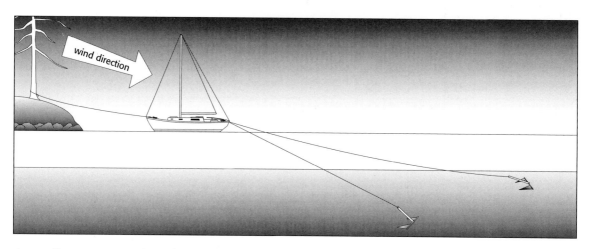

An excellent arrangement for anchoring out: bow to windward, tied to a sturdy tree, and two widely separated, deeply embedded anchors at the stern.

often two—situated to take the strain as the wind shifts direction and the boat swings to face into it.

If you are on your boat in a minor storm, you may have an opportunity during a lull to make some adjustments. If the rode is chafing, you can adjust the length of the rode or replace the chafing gear. If need be, you can even use the engine to head the boat into the wind. But it is almost impossible to employ any of these strategies when the wind is over 40 to 45 miles per hour. And in a major storm, the last place you should be is on your boat

BELIEVERS IN ANCHORING OUT

Fran and Shirley McGoldrick and their African gray parrot, Sinbad, are year-round liveaboards on *Ariel*, a 41-foot Formosa ketch. They cruise in southern waters during the winter and spend their summers on the Delaware River north of Philadelphia. It has always been their style to avoid staying at marinas and pass their nights on the hook. There are few situations, except a direct hit from a hurricane, that they haven't experienced. Anchoring night after night along the Georgia and Florida coastlines has taught them many lessons on what works and what doesn't.

Ariel weighs 38,000 pounds and carries an all-chain rode leading from an anchor windlass out over a bow roller. In the waters they cruise, a 66-pound Bruce primary anchor, backed up by a 43-pound Danforth, have held through all types of weather, including a seemingly

endless night of 75 mph wind at the public anchorage in Wrightsville Beach, North Carolina. The anchors held again when the boat was moored, Bahamian style, in a raging current and wind in St. Augustine, Florida. Only near Solomons Island in Chesapeake Bay did the Bruce drag a few feet through a soupy, muddy bottom before quickly resetting itself.

Fran and Shirley's advice for anchoring when a bad storm approaches is to strip the boat of all canvas; remove the solar panels, wind instruments, and antennas; close the boat up tight; and let out as much scope as possible. They also remove the dinghy from its davits, tie it off the stern with chafe protection, and let it stream astern on the wind. Even if the dinghy swamps, it is safer than hanging from the davits. Then, they leave the boat and hope for the best.

10 Preparing Your Boat

Once you've properly secured your boat on a mooring, at anchor, in a slip, at a dock, or in a narrow waterway, your next job is to prepare it to minimize damage or loss from two hazards: water intrusion through vents, hatches, ports, and through-hulls; and wind damage to exposed gear. We'll also discuss preparing boats stored on land, where inland flooding, storm surge, wind, and flying debris raise special issues.

PREVENTING WATER INTRUSION

First let's look at keeping water where it belongs—outside your boat. And to do this, you'll need to protect your boat on several fronts. For starters, the torrential rains of a hurricane can sink a boat. A slow-moving storm can dump 10, 15, even 20 inches of rain and more. (In 2005, Hurricane Ophelia dumped 12 inches of rain on my boat in less than 12 hours.) Water can also enter the boat below the waterline via through-hulls and breaches in the hull, and above the waterline—driven by the wind—through vents, hatches, and ports. Following are steps you should take to ensure your boat stays dry.

Charge the boat's batteries. If water enters the bilge for hours on end, causing the bilge pumps to run continuously, eventually, the batteries will run out of juice. Give your boat a fighting chance by making sure the batteries have a full charge before the storm begins.

Check where your bilge pump discharges. It is possible for a pump that discharges close to the waterline to backflow when waves or heeling from wind put the drains underwater. To avoid this, connect a long hose to the pump outlet so it discharges higher up—perhaps just over the gunwale.

Clean the bilge of all debris that could clog the bilge pump. The last thing you need is for the pump to clog because a length of oil-soaked line or a paper label from a can of beans was sucked into the intake.

Have a manual auxiliary pump onboard. It may come in handy when you return to the boat after the storm and find water has entered.

Close all through-hull connections. Be sure to either label them as closed or write yourself a note to that effect. This will prevent you from later starting the engine with the through-hull seacocks closed.

You should have a diagram showing where all through-hull connections are located, including fittings for the head, sinks, engine cooling, and air conditioner. If your boat didn't come with a through-hull diagram from the dealer, making your own is a good project for the off-season.

Don't plug your cockpit drains or scuppers. You want them to work. This is a good time, however, to inspect all cockpit drain fittings, both at the deck level and at the through-hull, to make sure they're sound and secure.

Cover vent openings. Winds can be so strong in a major storm that the boat will heel over far enough to put the side ventilators underwater. High winds may also drive water right through the engine vents, so tape over small vents, including fuel and water tank vents on the side of the hull. Screw a piece of plywood over larger vents or cowls using proper gasket material to ensure a good seal.

Plug the engine exhausts with cork or Styrofoam. If you're tied up in a fixed position and not swinging at an anchor or mooring, a wind shift could expose your stern to the full force of the gale. Plugging the engine exhausts will prevent water from entering. Put this on your list of closed through-hulls so you don't try to start the engine with the plugs in place after the storm.

Dog down all opening ports and hatches. Large glass windows hold up surprisingly well in heavy winds—better than Plexiglas, which bends more, thus opening up gaps at the gaskets and letting water through. Regardless, seal the edges of *all* windows, doors, and hatches with duct tape. Use window covers if you have them and tape around the edges.

Cover all dorade vents. If your anchor well is not self-draining, tape it over or stuff a heavy rag or terry cloth towel into the hawsepipe. Check the deck carefully to be sure you haven't missed any openings.

After the storm, remove the tape as soon as possible to prevent the transfer of sticky stuff to the boat surface. If there is some residue, try Goo Gone, which should remove the mess. WD-40 also seems to work well.

Remove exterior electronics. Covers on your exterior-mounted electronics are not watertight, so all electronics that *can* be removed *should* be removed. This includes radar monitors, GPS receivers, radios, and depth finders.

Protect "permanent" electronics with duct tape. You may have equipment that is more or less permanently installed in the instrument panel or so inaccessible that it is all but impossible to take out. For these items, place duct tape over the face of the equipment, the switches, and all edges where the equipment faceplate or enclosure meets the cabinetry. Overlap each strip of tape for a watertight seal, starting at the bottom and working your way up so that the overlaps shed water like clapboards. Pay special attention to your main electrical panel: seal it completely so moisture can't get in and short out the electrical system.

PREVENTING WIND DAMAGE

Strong winds are your enemy. Even if a boat is properly secured in a slip or canal, a strong enough wind can heel it over so far that it ships water over the gunwales. Boats on dry land can be tipped over or even lifted off the ground and tossed around. An anchor or mooring can fail if the boat has too much surface area exposed to the wind. Wind can bend or break any number of a boat's appendages and will almost certainly lift anything not fastened down and blow it away.

Remove all gear that creates additional exposed surface area. It is a lot of work to remove dinghies, life rings, booms, antennas, outriggers, solar panels, Plexiglas windscreens, biminis, and canvas covers, but the reduction in windage is appreciable. For example, the tower top or bimini on a sportfisherman will act as a sail and could ultimately capsize the boat if it heels over from a strong wind. Remove them if possible.

Beyond the windage issue, almost all of these items can themselves be damaged by high winds. All boat canvas—enclosures, biminis, dodgers, etc.—will be among the first to go, although radio and radar antennas, outriggers, and the like are also at significant risk.

If you can't take all the removed canvas, sails, antennas, etc., home or to storage, arrange them as neatly as possible down below. Don't just sling them on a bunk or in the passageway; they could seriously compromise your cleanup or recovery operations after the storm.

To reduce damage and windage, remove everything that can be removed. This includes solar panels, canvas, wind instruments, antennas, rack-stored fenders, life rings, dinghies, and more. (Courtesy FEMA)

This boat might have survived at anchor if the owner had removed the windage-producing canvas dodger and top hamper. (Courtesy FEMA)

Remove unattached objects above-deck. This includes deck furniture, cushions (even if they are held down with snaps), folding swim ladders, fender racks, life rafts, dinghies, life rings, spinnaker poles, boat hooks, barbecue grills, small outboard motors, bicycles, sailboards, and any unused anchors that are on deck.

One exception: If you are in a marina or yacht club, it is a good idea to leave some extra docking lines in the cockpit. Tag them with a notation of their length, which may help emergency personnel select the right one to replace a lost dock line.

Toss a few extra docking lines into the cockpit so the marina staff has lines at the ready if needed in an emergency.

Remove items belowdeck. Go below and strip the boat of everything possible. This includes anything that could be damaged by water intrusion (e.g., portable electronics, clothing, cushions, bedding, charts, books, owner's manuals, radio license, logbook, and registration papers), and anything that might be lost to looters (e.g., tools and any portable boat gear and valuables) should things turn really nasty. Take it all home and place it in a safe, dry place.

As you leave the boat, put duct tape over the companionway door jamb.

Don't forget the dock box. Ideally, the dock box should be through-bolted to the dock—something to take care of at the beginning of the boating season. If, as is more likely, it's just sitting unattached on the dock, secure it with lines or remove it to a safer place. It's a good idea to remove anything of value.

Ideally, take your dinghy home. The dinghy storage area is probably the last place marina personnel will address in their efforts to secure the yard. Most dinghy racks are pretty flimsy affairs and are not to be trusted. Putting the dinghy in your garage is undoubtedly the safest choice. If you have to leave it outside, either at home or at the yard, fill it with water to make sure the wind doesn't catch it and blow it away. However, this is not an option if the dinghy will be in a low-lying area that might flood. In that case, turn it upside down and tie it to deadmen (anchors embedded in the ground) or some other immovable object.

This dinghy is well secured, although it would be safer to just take it home.

The owner of this boat has stripped the canvas and sails in preparation for a storm. A few more well-placed spring lines, and removing the outboard, cooking grill, and radome, would also be a good idea.

SPECIAL PREPARATIONS FOR SAILBOATS

Sailboat owners have a few more specialized tasks to accomplish:

Remove all sail covers and sails, including the roller furling headsail. Roller furling is almost guaranteed to unfurl in high winds and cause rigging damage at the very least. It could even power the boat enough to drive it into pilings, break it loose from the mooring, or drag the anchor.

Remove spinnaker poles, whisker poles, and every other spar possible, including the boom. If you can't remove the boom, loosen the topping lift so that the end of the boom rests on the deck, then lash the end securely to the stern cleats. Tighten down the vang. If your mast is on a tabernacle, lower it and tie it down securely.

Tie the halyard shackles to the rail tightly if the halyards cannot be removed. Alternatively, tie all the halyards on each mast together securely and run them up to the top of the mast with a single messenger line that can be secured to the rail. Windage will be greatly reduced and halyard flogging all but eliminated. After the storm, the messenger line can be used to bring the halyards back to the deck.

Storm preparations in progress. These boatowners have chosen not to remove their sails but instead to wrap lines around the canvas covers. The topping lifts have been removed and the booms have been tied down. If time permits, the owner of the boat on the left should remove the outboard motor and the propane tanks.

PREPARATIONS FOR LAND STORAGE

Almost every piece of advice that applies to boats stored in the water is relevant to boats stored on land. You still need to prevent water intrusion through vents, windows, hatches, and exhaust pipes. Windage is as much a hazard on dry land as it is in the water. Seal all openings and strip the boat of everything that can add to windage, blow away, be ruined by rain, or stolen.

Although this boat is tied down to anchors in the ground and the wheels are chocked, a strong wind will likely tear off the canvas cover. The boat is small enough to be put somewhere indoors with the mast down, which would be safer.

Trailer Storage

If your boat will be on a trailer, secure it to the trailer with as many tie-downs as possible. Put blocks under the wheels and let some air out of the tires to stabilize the trailer. Or, if available, secure the trailer to deadmen anchors or rebar buried about 2

A boat on a trailer is somewhat top-heavy to begin with and doesn't need a huge amount of wind to flip it over. Although this boat was well secured to its trailer, the trailer itself should have been tied to anchors in the ground. (Courtesy FEMA)

feet deep in the ground. Smaller boats can be taken off their trailers and tied directly to these buried anchors.

Some trailer boat owners close the drain plug, turn off the bilge pump, and partially fill their boats with water to add weight. Before taking this course of action, carefully examine the lower portions of your boat's interior to determine how far it can be filled without causing damage to electronics or upholstery. It's not a good idea to fill the bilge up to that maximum "safe" level, because water intrusion from a downpour could easily raise the level by several inches. Also consider the possibility of damage to wood-cored structures from prolonged immersion. If you do add water, put blocks between the springs and the frame of the trailer to support the extra weight. This is a good idea in any case, since water may get into the boat during the storm.

Lift Storage

If at all possible, remove your boat from a shoreside lift. If you must leave the boat on a lift, remove the bilge drain plug to prevent the additional weight of rainwater from collapsing the lift, and strap down the boat securely. It's also a good idea to remove the outboard. Of course, lifts should be carefully maintained year-round, both to retain their structural integrity and to ensure that you can launch your boat quickly if you choose to leave.

Yard Storage

Some boatowners and many marinas feel that yard storage is the best defensive position against storm damage. In many cases, this is because the boat won't have to rely on the integrity of lines, cleats, anchors, and other such fallible hardware (and your ability to arrange it all properly). But before you haul your boat, determine if the yard

A storm surge of just a few feet could dislodge this boat from the lift. The weight of the outboard engine makes the arrangement unbalanced and stern heavy, which will only make matters worse.

This badly rusted lift-turning rod will seriously compromise the lift's ability to withstand a strong storm. A heavy strain or rocking of the boat in the wind could easily break the ¼-inch steel and drop the boat.

has ample elevation above the maximum potential storm surge or other sources of flooding. If the yard is too low, flooding could destroy almost everything.

Flying debris is another hazard of yard storage. Most marinas have plenty of lightweight materials scattered about that can easily become airborne missiles and cause a great deal of damage to hulls and topsides.

If you choose yard storage for a large boat, use at least four jack stands on each side. Each stand should rest on a pad of thick plywood and have a chain running under the keel to its opposite member. Strip the boat of all loose items and windage, just as you would for in-water storage, and close it up as tight as possible. Keep shrink-wrap in place, but remove tarp covers, as it's nearly impossible to secure them adequately. If you insist on leaving a tarp in place, secure it with a superabundance of lines, and do *not* tie those lines to the jack stands. A flapping tarp will pull the jack stands right out from under your boat, and over it will go!

For small sailboats, remove the mast and boom, place the boat on the ground upside down, and tie it securely to deadmen.

If your boat will be in dry-stack storage, secure your boat in the racks (if the marina allows it). Few if any dry-stack marinas allow customers to climb the racks to strap their boats securely to the structure, so the strapping-down option is pretty much limited to boats on the ground floor. If your boat is normally kept on an upper level, try and have it relocated to the bottom tier, or have it placed on your trailer and remove it to a secure location. If the boat must weather the storm on an upper level in a dry slip, add as much weight as possible without giving the wind anything to catch. You can at least fill your fuel and water tanks. Some owners also put filled water jugs in the cockpit.

INVENTORY AND DOCUMENTATION

No matter where you place your boat prior to the storm, thoroughly document your preparations in case you need proof for an insurance claim. Take photos or make a video to document how you secured the boat, including all the lines, jack stands, supports, or straps used. After you have stripped the boat of everything removable, photograph the interior to show the remaining items. Show the cabins, saloon, galley, and head from every angle, and open up hatches and cabinets to include their contents. Show every measure you took against water intrusion (closed seacocks, plugged exhaust pipes, and taped-over ports, hatches, and vents, etc.).

If you're taking photos, a wide-angle lens setting (14 mm to 20 mm) is helpful for interior shots. If you're videotaping, a voice-over commentary can add details that might be missed in a purely visual presentation.

If your photographs or video show that all due diligence was taken, there should be no room for a difference of opinion or a claim of negligence.

Recovering and Restoring Your Boat

Long before storm season begins, assemble your storm-recovery kit. If you also use some of the items around the home, make a checklist to ensure these final items are added to the kit before you return to your boat after the storm. As you hunker down in your home, waiting for the storm to abate and for your marina to become accessible, you can pull the final items together. The following list shows the items that you'll want to include in your kit:

STORM RECOVERY AND CLEANING SUPPLIES

Work gloves

Safety glasses or goggles

Bolt cutters, to clear away broken or damaged cables, shrouds, or wire halyards

A large container of Marine-Tex epoxy putty to seal small leaks or cracks in fiberglass

Duct tape

Cleaning compounds like Fantastik, Windex, and Castrol Super Clean

Anticorrosion spray like CRC Heavy Duty Corrision Inhibitor

Scrub brush

Broom

Rags, cloth towels, paper towels, and newspapers

Shovel

Heavy-duty garbage bags

Tarps and/or plastic sheeting (including a small tarp with tie-down grommets to cover a possible hole in the hull)

Bailing buckets

Plywood

Tool kit (hammer, saws, screwdrivers, pliers, wrenches, wire cutters, pry bars, etc.)

Fasteners (screws, nails)

Electric fans and power cords
First-aid kit

WHEN TO GO TO YOUR BOAT

Stay tuned to the local radio stations or NOAA weather radio right after the storm as they will broadcast bridge reopenings, announcements of clearance for people to reenter evacuated areas, and of course, weather advisories.

To aid this process further, as part of your storm preparations, make a list that includes the telephone numbers and Internet addresses of local government offices and media outlets. Then if you have to evacuate, you'll be able to obtain local reentry

LESSONS LEARNED: HOPE FOR THE FUTURE

When Hurricane Ivan slammed ashore near the Florida-Alabama state line in September 2004, the storm's 120 mph winds and 15-foot storm surge left a path of smashed buildings, eroded beaches, and buckled roads in its wake. But as bad as it was, should it have taken 3 weeks for the last evacuees to be allowed back home?

Officials in Florida quickly realized that while their evacuation plans worked well, their reentry plans hadn't kept up with the area's tremendous population growth. The return migration was a disorganized mass of people trying to get back to their homes, businesses, and boats. The results were long lines of angry people with frayed nerves and totally overwhelmed officials.

The issues resulting from the lack of planning with Hurricane Ivan should have led to better preparations for future storms, but sadly they didn't. All we need do is look at the disaster caused by poor planning before, during, and after Hurricane Katrina in 2005; the mandatory evacuation of New Orleans was ordered too late, and little provision was made for the thousands of people without transportation, who were then stranded in the flooded, lawless city; tens of thousands were left homeless; and thousands died. We can only hope that the total breakdown of city, state, and federal agencies will lead to the development of better cooperative procedures in the future.

The problems experienced during and after Hurricane Ivan in 2004 and Hurricane Katrina in 2005 will hopefully make future reentry problems and possible solutions more obvious to city, state, and federal officials throughout the nation. Not only does forecasting get better year after year, but emergency response authorities continue to learn how to better prepare.

One of the keys that improves reentry plans is disseminating more accurate and updated information. Close cooperation between local, county, and state governments is essential to ensure that official announcements are both accurate and consistent. Cooperation between government and broadcast media is also essential. And if the storm has not forced a mass evacuation to distant locations, public meetings can be useful (held as soon as possible after the storm passes and in a location near to, but not within, the immediate damage zone). At these meetings, every aspect of the recovery effort can be discussed and debated with the public.

Using sightseeing trolleys to tour accessible areas and enable property owners to get at least a preliminary view of the damage before full access is permitted is a possibility. Another option is broadcasting low-level aerial reconnaissance over local TV and posted on government websites to allow viewers a bird's-eye view of areas that are not yet accessible.

For coastal boatowners who live out of state, however, it is a challenge to get information to them before they start their journey to a disaster area to inspect their boats for damage.

Sanibel Island, Florida, a barrier island on the Gulf Coast populated with expensive houses and boats, was hit hard by Hurricane Charley in 2004. Before the storm struck, officials set up a virtual city hall on the city's website (they used a generator to make sure the site's server remained up) to disseminate reentry and recovery information. The Internet allowed Sanibel officials to reach residents who had evacuated beyond the reach of the region's traditional media outlets such as the local newspaper, radio, and TV.

information that will not be carried on national media outlets. It will help speed up your ability to get to your boat as soon as it is safe and legal to do so, and also help minimize anxiety and frustration while waiting for access.

Don't attempt to return to your marina or anchorage until the authorities announce that it is safe to do so. Wires may be down and roads may be flooded. Even when access is permitted, expect to be challenged by police or National Guard. Be prepared to show your marina contract or some other proof of boat ownership to demonstrate your need for access to a storm-damaged area.

CLEANING UP AND REPAIRING DAMAGE

When you're finally able to gain access to your boat, be cautious and alert for dangerous situations. For example:

- Do a walkaround before boarding your boat. Look for exterior damage and potential dangers (e.g., from falling debris or downed wires).
- If your boat is on jack stands, make sure they're still securely in place.
- Be very careful when entering damaged boathouses or grounded boats and when working around floating debris. There will be nails in boards, window frames with broken glass, and no end of dangerous possibilities floating on or just under the surface.
- Report any gas, oil, or chemical spills to marina management, the Coast Guard, and local authorities; this is a serious legal obligation for every boatowner.
- If you do find a spill, take immediate action to prevent further discharge.
- Do not hook up to the electrical and water connections until marina management has given the okay.
- Watch out for snakes, rodents, and other wildlife, as well as lost or abandoned pets, all of which may have been traumatized by the storm and driven to higher ground.
- Finally, help your neighbors. You may have had little damage, due to your prestorm efforts, but some of them may be in real trouble and need all the help they can get.

Photograph or Videotape the Boat

As soon as you are sure the boat condition is stable, and before you begin to clean up, photograph or videotape its condition inside and out to document any damage. A comparison to the same shots you took prior to the storm will assist the insurance company in making a fair settlement. A photograph may also later reveal damage you might have missed in your first, frantic walk-through.

In the shots you take, both before and after the storm, include a close-up of the day's newspaper or set the camera to print the date to confirm the time of the images.

Check for Chafe

If the boat weathered the storm successfully in the water, examine the docking, mooring, or anchor lines for chafe. There could be another storm on the way within days, and you want those lines to do as good a job during the next one as they did during the last one. A series of damaging storms will allow you little time for replacing lines and upgrading chafing gear, but you must beware the risk of complacency. In Florida in 2004, boatowners who survived early storms often made comments like, "That one wasn't so bad. The boat did fine." When their boats were damaged by a subsequent hurricane, they regretted not taking more precautions.

Check for Leaks

Look for rust spots and water stains where you've never seen them before. Check around belowdeck for wet spots where a hatch may have sprung, allowing a leak. If a hatch has sprung, it should be taped over and repaired as soon as possible. Get down on your hands and knees and examine the carpet for wet spots. If it's wet, remove it to dry elsewhere, and search assiduously until you find the source of the leak. Check in lazarettes, cabinets, under seating, and any place that is hidden from sight.

If any water entered the boat, open all the hatches, ports and companionways to get fresh, drying air belowdeck as soon as weather permits. Wipe down every hard surface of the interior to remove dirt and salt residue. Set up fans if you have power. Clean the bilge and be sure the bilge pump strainers are clear.

Disconnect the batteries before attempting to dry the electrical panel. Then check the electric panel connections to be sure they are dry. Corrosion will surely occur if the panel and its wiring have gotten wet. Before you reconnect the shore-power cables from the power source on shore and physically dry the connections. Then spray them with a water displacing, corrosion inhibitor like CRC Heavy Duty Corrosion Inhibitor.

Remove the Water

Before the storm, you did all you could to prepare for a potential leak (as we discussed in Chapter 10). But in spite of your preparations, you may find a leak that the bilge pumps are failing to keep up with. Hopefully, you've brought a helper along, and you can immediately assign him or her to begin operating the manual bilge pump while you search for the source of the leak and attempt to stop it. If necessary, try and solicit the help of people nearby to help bail with buckets or go for help. The marina may have a large-capacity pump they can use to assist you. Other possible sources of help may include the harbormaster, fire department, or Coast Guard, although don't depend too heavily on them—they're likely to be pretty busy.

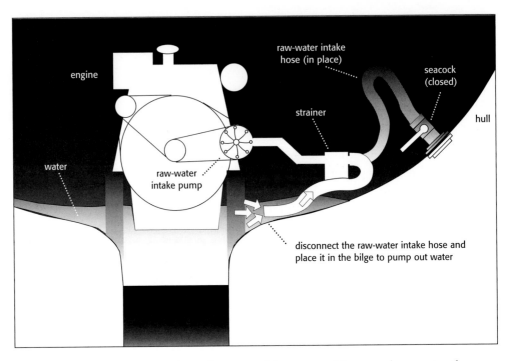

raw-water intake
hose (in place)

seacock
(closed)

engine

strainer

hull

water

raw-water
intake pump

disconnect the raw-water intake hose and
place it in the bilge to pump out water

Your engine's raw-water pump can be used as a powerful emergency bilge pump by removing the hose from the through-hull. Remember to close the valve first!

Excess water in the bilge will affect the boat's stability and may make it more susceptible to capsizing in heavy wind and waves. Be cautious, and get out of the boat fast if there is the least possibility of capsizing or sinking.

Your boat probably has an emergency pump aboard that you may not have even thought about: the engine's raw-water pump. If your bilge pumps aren't making sufficient headway against incoming water, shut the cooling water intake seacock, remove the intake hose from the seacock, and place the end in the bilge. Make sure that engine and exhaust vents are opened up and unplugged, then crank up the engine and allow the water pump to do its work. Be extremely careful not to suck up debris from the bilge; it could clog your engine's cooling passages and damage the pump. Also make sure you shut down the engine before it runs out of "coolant" in the bilge.

With some preseason preparation, you can make this procedure faster and more secure. Between the through-hull seacock and the seawater strainer, install a Y-valve, or diverter, and connect a length of hose to the Y-valve's free leg to reach the deepest point of the bilge. Place some kind of screen or strainer over the end of the bilge hose, and wire the Y-valve in position with stainless steel wire to draw water through the through-hull. In an emergency, cut the wire and switch the Y-valve over to pull water from the bilge.

Find the Leak

Now that you've done everything you can to remove water from the boat, begin your search for the source of the leak. (Of course, if the leak was a large one, you would have sought it out and plugged it before trying to remove the water. If the boat had a major leak, it probably sank; see the If Your Boat Sank section next page.)

If the problem is a damaged hose at a through-hull that you failed to close prior to the storm, merely closing the through-hull valve will probably do the trick until you can replace the hose. If the valve itself is damaged, remove the hose and hammer a wood plug of the right size into the stem of the through-hull.

However, the flooding may be caused by a hole in the hull. Use rags, towels, cushions, bedding, clothing, pillows—anything that can be forced into the hole—to reduce the flow of water to the point where the bilge pumps can make some progress. If possible, apply the plastic tarp with grommets (that is part of your recovery kit) to the outside of the hole where the pressure of the water will help press it against the hull. Using the grommets, tie the tarp as tightly as possible across the hole; if necessary, pass lines under the boat to pull the lower part of the tarp down.

But the leak may come from one of those mystery places that are harder to identify. Check the hull construction joints, keel bolts, and any other possible point of water entry. If the leak is small enough, a fast-setting, underwater epoxy putty like Marine-Tex may be all that is necessary.

IF YOUR BOAT IS AGROUND

A boat aground, whether hard aground, lying in shallow water, or up against a retaining wall, is bad news. Hulls are not designed to support themselves without the upward and inward pressure of the water they float in (or resting on their keel and stabilized by well-configured jack stands on land), and they're certainly not designed to lie on their sides against rocks, whether or not they're being pummeled by waves.

If the boat is not badly holed, you should patch any small breaks and refloat it as quickly as possible. Unfortunately, large boats can't be moved easily, and the heavy equipment that can move them is likely to be in strong demand following a bad storm. Even small boats are difficult or impossible to move without proper lifting or towing equipment. But you may be able to prevent further damage, depending on how the boat was grounded.

A boat grounded in shallow water, or the intertidal zone, is in the worst situation. It will be subject to tides that may lift it and set it down again, perhaps in someplace even worse, and to waves that may pummel it against the rocks. Tie the boat off to anchors embedded far ashore or to trees so that the high tide doesn't float it off, then do all you can to repair any holes or leaks, and have it pulled off as soon as possible.

A boat sitting on its side on dry land just above the high tide line is better off with its bottom facing to seaward, so that waves at high tide don't drive water against the deck

Boats stranded in the intertidal zone must be removed as quickly as possible to avoid further damage from pounding waves. But since every mobile crane operator in the vicinity is likely to be busy in the aftermath of a major storm, you may have to wait in line. (Courtesy FEMA)

and through hatches or companionways. If possible, roll or turn the boat using come-alongs, a block and tackle, wrecking bars, rollers, and similar tools of mechanical advantage. Put cushions and fenders between the hull and the ground for protection if you can.

IF YOUR BOAT SANK

If your boat sank, contact your insurance agent immediately so that a surveyor can be dispatched to assess the damage. Many fully submerged boats are considered total losses, as the cost of refurbishing them is often more than the insurance coverage. Partially submerged boats have a good probability of being brought back to original condition within the realm of reasonable economics.

In either case, decisions should be made quickly since machinery submerged in salt water corrodes quickly. Freshwater submersions, though serious, are usually not as costly to repair.

Pickling Your Engine

If the boat sank in salt water, you can expect that the engines and electronics will need to be rebuilt or replaced. Because corrosion begins as soon as the boat is exposed to air, the best approach is to leave the boat submerged until a qualified mechanic is available to spend an afternoon working on it to begin the pickling process. If that isn't possible, and your boat has been raised, you will have to *pickle* it—remove all the water, and coat every passageway, cavity, and recess inside the engine with diesel fuel—yourself. (Diesel fuel is used, even with gasoline engines, because it does a good job of coating the inside surfaces.)

To pickle an engine, follow these steps:

1. Disconnect all batteries and shore power.
2. Hit the engine with a hard spray of fresh water from a hose. Wash it down well to remove all the exterior mud, debris, and salt.

3. Remove the alternator and starter and flush fresh water into every crevice and opening. Dry them with towels and set them in the sun to dry completely.
4. Remove the engine's sump drain plug and drain as much of the water as possible into a container for proper disposal.
5. Remove all the injectors or spark plugs.
6. Place lots of oil-absorbing pads around the engine and replace the drain plug.
7. Fill the engine with diesel fuel through the air intake or carburetor until the diesel fuel overflows. This overflow will bring the internal water with it.
8. Turn over the engine by hand several times with a wrench to distribute the diesel fuel everywhere inside the engine. This will blow the water out of the cylinders along with some diesel fuel.
9. Add more diesel fuel, again until it overflows, and repeat step 8.
10. When the oil-absorbing pads become saturated, replace them with fresh ones, being sure to bag and discard the saturated ones responsibly.

You have now successfully pickled your engine. This process will give you enough time to bring in a qualified mechanic to make all the necessary repairs to the engine, starter, alternator, and wiring. The pickling should last for quite a while, but I would not hope for much success at rejuvenating a sunk engine if the pickling is more than 4 weeks old.

Once all the above has been done, it can't hurt to use a preservative spray like CRC Heavy Duty Corrosion Inhibitor all over the exterior of the engine.

Electrical Equipment

Much of the electrical equipment on a sunk boat will also need replacing, though the wiring will probably be reusable as water does not migrate into the insulation beyond the ends of the terminals. Once you have cut off the damaged terminal ends and made new connections, the wires should be fully functional. But do replace shore-power cables and battery cables as their factory-sealed fittings can be damaged by immersion.

Finally, check everything else on the boat to be sure all traces of sinking have been addressed. Check for bent aluminum towers by sighting along the tubes. Examine all welds and fittings carefully for cracks. Don't overlook hidden places like door hinges, fixtures, drawer slides, and exposed screw heads. Galley equipment and head accessories should be thoroughly cleaned and lubricated as needed.

If any cushions, bedding and clothing were left on board and are salvageable, put them outside to dry.

12 Marine Salvage

Salvage—a legal concept recognized by admiralty law for more than 3,000 years—entitles a party to a reward for saving a vessel in peril. Professional salvors aren't the only ones who can make a claim for a salvage award; passing boaters who lend a hand (known as chance salvors) are also entitled to a reward.

The idea that salvage applies only for rescuing a large commercial ship is a myth. Salvage can be claimed for something as trivial as towing a small sailboat off a beach. The law applies to every vessel in navigable waters, from rowboats to oceangoing tankers. If you find yourself in a salvage situation, make sure to contact your insurer and/or a marine attorney knowledgeable about the law of salvage. Use the information in this chapter as a general introduction only.

Until recently, recreational boaters had little reason to be concerned with salvage. If your boat was in distress or grounded, all you had to do was call the U.S. Coast Guard, who would come to your assistance. But because of budget restrictions and changes in policy and mission, the Coast Guard no longer provides nonemergency assistance when commercial help is available. If there is no danger to the persons involved, and as long as commercial assistance can be obtained, the Coast Guard will not respond.

THE CONCEPT OF PERIL

If you find yourself grounded on a sandbar and a salvor pulls you off, his action can be considered a salvage operation, not just a tow, as your boat may be legally considered to be in peril.

Danger to a boat does not have to be immediate, imminent, or absolute for the concept of peril to apply. For a salvor to claim an award, the only requirement is that the boat has encountered danger, misfortune, or other situations that expose it to damage or destruction if the salvage service is not provided. Therefore, a boat on the beach exposed to the wind, waves, and weather is in peril as further damage and even total loss *may* ensue. Almost any boat aground on a falling tide could suffer damage when the weight of the hull is no longer supported by the water. Peril of any sort, whether imminent or potential, supports a claim for salvage services. The amount of danger is not the issue. Slight, moderate, or extreme peril affects the amount of the salvor's award; it does not negate the fact that the salvor is entitled to a salvage award.

TOWING AND SALVAGE

There are important differences between towing and salvage. Towing is a service that is done in the absence of peril. Often this results from dead batteries, engine failure, running out of fuel, or a soft grounding where there is no immediate danger. Towing is also defined as one tow vessel and one tow line. A typical towing charge is based on hourly rates.

Salvage operations may occur when a boat is sinking, hard aground, stranded, or on fire, and it involves removing the boat from the accident site. If there is immediate danger to the subject boat, the environment, or other vessels, it is a salvage operation. Other possible requirements that turn a towing operation into a salvage service are when pumps or flotation devices are employed to protect the boat, and two tow lines and/or two tow vessels are used.

Salvage work cannot be performed if the owner of a boat refuses the salvor's services. But if a boat is exposed to peril, and no one is on board to refuse or accept the salvor's offered services, the salvor is not required to locate the boatowner before performing a salvage operation. Boatowners have tried to deny salvage claims by asserting that the salvors were trespassing, but such assertions have not held up in admiralty courts. If salvage is performed in the absence of the owner's refusal, the claim is valid.

There is a popular belief that a derelict boat found adrift or abandoned becomes the property of the finder. This is not true. An abandoned boat remains the property of her owner. A salvor who brings the boat to a safe port can claim the right to a salvage award, but not to ownership.

Salvage Awards

Though salvage may seem like a harsh concept, salvage operations often cost insurance companies and boatowners less than wreck removal plus the value of the loss.

For a salvor to claim a salvage reward, the operation in general must comply with three basic circumstances: marine peril must exist; the service must be performed voluntarily on the part of the salvor; and the salvor must be successful in saving people and/or property.

Salcon 89—an international agreement signed by the United States at the Salvage Convention in 1989—defines ten criteria that must be considered in determining the amount of a salvage award:

1. The salvaged value of the vessel.
2. The skill level of the salvors in preventing or minimizing damage to the environment.

3. The amount of success from the salvage operation.
4. The nature and degree of the dangers involved.
5. The skill and effort of the salvors.
6. Time and expense incurred by the salvors.
7. The risk of liability and other risks run by the salvor.
8. The promptness of the service.
9. The availability and use of vessels and other equipment used.
10. The state of readiness and efficiency of the salvor's equipment.

On arriving at your marina or yard with your boat in tow, a successful salvor will place a lien on your boat until the salvage costs are paid. According to Salcon 89, the marina or yard may not legally release your boat after repairs have been finished until the lien has been paid.

Most marine insurance policies provide coverage for salvage of the vessel and should issue a bond to the salvor after the repairs are complete, which allows for the release of the boat to the owner.

Sometimes, after the salvage is completed, the boat saved is determined to be a total loss (from an insurance point of view), and the salvage value of the boat is not sufficient to pay the award. In this case, the salvor is generally entitled to no compensation, as he has salvaged nothing of value. However, in the case of a salvage operator who prevents oil pollution, there is a possibility the salvor can receive an award under a special compensation provision of Salcon 89.

A Boatowner's Options

What can you do as a boatowner to lessen the potential for a misunderstanding between a simple towing job and a salvage operation?

Purchasing a comprehensive marine insurance policy and engaging, under contract, a reputable towing company is the first step. Be sure there is towing coverage in your insurance policy. It's also a good idea to become a member of a towing organization; remember to renew your membership each year.

If the towing company has an existing contract to perform work, it cannot present a salvage claim. As noted above, for salvage to apply, the service must be voluntary on the part of the service provider. By "voluntary," the law means that there is no pre-existing contractual agreement between the salvor and the vessel in distress. If a contract is in place, the service isn't voluntary, it's an obligation. However, most towing service contracts only cover normal towing for normal, garden-variety groundings. If a normal tow can't get you off and extraordinary measures of some sort are required (such as the use of a crane, or repairs to the hull prior to moving the boat), then it is probably not covered by the standard towing contract and a salvage situation may exist. Look carefully at your towing contract to determine if it covers all your possible needs.

A towing contract can eliminate the problem of having a salvage situation. (Courtesy Sea Tow Services International)

Your insurance company should help you deal with salvage expenses, including assisting in any binding arbitration and/or litigation in a maritime court. Unfortunately, some insurance companies try to avoid these legal expenses by attempting to persuade an uninformed insured boatowner to engage in the legal process single-handed. Your best defense against the occasional unscrupulous insurer is to learn as much as possible about salvage concepts and your insurance coverage, and press your agent for clarification and action on your loss.

Be certain that you have full vessel value in your salvage coverage. You don't want a policy that covers only a percentage of the boat's value, nor do you want a deductible. The full value of wreck removal should also be stipulated in the policy, again with no deductible.

If possible, consult with your insurance company before allowing a salvage operation to take place. This is only feasible where a small delay will not increase the possibility of damage to the boat. When more immediate action is necessary, try to avoid a salvage situation by establishing the nature of the service as a tow. Before you hand a line over to a tow boat, ask, "Is this salvage or a tow?" If you do not have a contract with the tow operator, ask for a fixed price in writing. And if that's not feasible, have any verbal agreement witnessed by one of your crew. In the absence of a signed contract it is difficult to resolve disputes in arbitration, and disagreements often lead to court action. If time permits and the operator offering a tow gives you any reason to doubt the situation, you can refuse his services and contact a reputable towing company.

As the above implies, one of the best strategies is to have a prenegotiated, fixed-price towing contract before any loss occurs. While there are occasional abuses by salvors, these usually are from by fly-by-night operators; salvage operators more often provide a valuable service to those with boats in distress.

13 Storm Stories from Hurricane Hugo

Hurricane Hugo hit the Charleston, South Carolina, area on September 21, 1989. Few tropical cyclones up to that time had ever had lower barometric pressure, stronger winds, or higher storm surge at landfall. It was watched carefully from the time it developed off the Cape Verde Islands until it became a full-fledged hurricane.

A NOAA reconnaissance aircraft reached Hugo late on September 15 and penetrated the eye, expecting to find, as predicted, winds of 100 to 115 miles per hour. Instead, the crew recorded sustained winds of 190 mph and a barometric pressure of 918 millibars. The NOAA aircraft experienced such extreme buffeting that the aircraft was damaged, forcing the crew to dump 50,000 gallons of fuel while inside the eye. Satellite estimates had greatly underestimated the hurricane's strength. Based on these data, Hugo's surface winds were estimated at 160 mph, and it was rated as a Category 5 hurricane.

Hugo roared on, moving northwesterly over the Caribbean, causing incredible devastation, before it approached the Carolinas.

SURVIVAL AT ANCHOR

There are thousands of storm stories from Hugo, but few that are more harrowing than the experience of Larry Bramlett and his wife Mary, who rode out Hugo at anchor. The Bramletts lived over 500 miles from Charleston, but kept their boat in a slip at Stono Marina on Johns Island, just outside that city. Soon after they heard the news that Hurricane Hugo was headed toward the South Carolina coastline, friends at the marina called, saying that they were forming a flotilla of boats to go up the Cooper River as far as possible to get away from the coast. Larry and Mary said they'd be there as soon as they could, and arrived the day before the storm. Quickly preparing their 34-foot Morgan sloop, they joined the eight other boats for the journey 40 miles upriver to a spot the group had selected, just below the dam at Lake Moultrie, where navigable traffic ends.

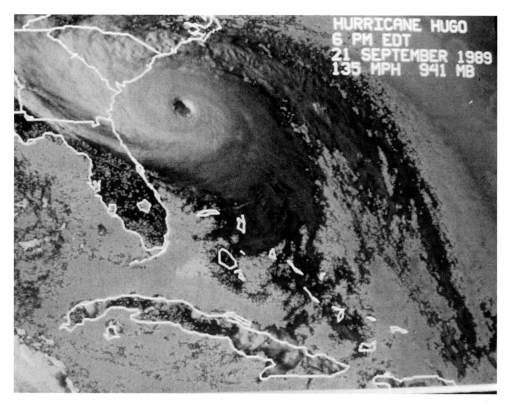

Hurricane Hugo bearing down on South Carolina, September 21, 1989. (Courtesy NOAA)

Larry, Mary, and their friends were the fortunate ones. Boaters who started later found the Ben Sawyer Bridge, a swing bridge, outside Charleston had already closed to boat traffic when they got there. In fact, all six drawbridges in Charleston County and the surrounding counties stopped opening for boats at about the same time as a result of the governor's evacuation order. Those boaters, who were also heading to the Cooper River for the safety of their favorite hurricane spot, had to turn back to their marinas. At that point, they had little time to get ready and had to work frantically in the heavy rain and increasing winds.

On the way upriver, Larry prepared the boat the best he knew how. He had never been through anything like this and was doing what he could to follow the advice of some of the "old salts" of Charleston who had experienced previous storms.

The previous owner of his Morgan had fortunately upgraded the cleats and chocks. Larry stripped the mainsail and headsail and stored them below. He stowed life rings, the grill, and anything loose on deck below, then removed the boom and lashed it to the deck.

When the flotilla arrived at the chosen spot, they immediately spread out to allow maximum swinging room and went about setting anchors. Many trees lined the shore but because of the swift current, tying up to them wouldn't allow their boats to face upriver. At least the trees would be helpful in breaking the wind, or so they thought.

Larry had a 35-pound CQR and a 40-pound Danforth as his main anchors. He attached 60 feet of chain, which he had hauled to the marina in the trunk of his car, to each of his anchors. To the chain he attached 150 feet of ¾-inch, three-strand nylon rode. When his ground tackle was assembled, he went about setting the anchors off the bow at approximately 45 degrees from each other. Mary backed down to dig in the anchors. At full power, the anchor rode was so taut it almost sang, and the bow dipped down toward the water. Once the anchors were set, the swift downriver current held their bow upstream, facing the dam. Larry paid out the rodes to their limits and cleated them fast. He thought it would be a good idea to dive down and check the anchors to see if they were well set but, as he descended the ladder, he saw a 6-foot alligator swim by. Mary had always handled the wheel when they set anchor and was an expert, so rather than risk an encounter with the alligator, they agreed to trust the anchors to hold.

As an added precaution, Larry attached a 20-pound sentinel with a brass slide to each rode and lowered them on a lanyard to a few feet off the bottom. The sentinel's weight would hold each rode down low enough to absorb a lot of the shock and also reduce the angle of the rode.

Even though the bow chocks and cleats had been upgraded to a large size, he worried that they might not hold. The bow cleats were all that stood between safety and disaster. So he ran the rodes through the bow eyes, tied each off to a bow cleat, then ran the rode farther back along the side decks and tied it off at the big mainsail winch. Finally, he tied the tail of each rode to the rear cleats. Even if the bow cleats tore loose, the rodes would still be secured at the mainsail winch and the rear cleats.

Larry had a smaller Danforth that he attached to a stern bridle and set off the stern. If they dragged anchor or broke loose altogether, he hoped the stern anchor would at least slow them down by dragging across the bottom.

They put out every fender they had, closed up all the dorades, windows, ports, and anything else that looked like it might admit wind-driven water, and went below to weather the storm.

Hugo hit with screaming winds and pounding rain. The dam upstream released water at full force to prevent flooding farther inland, resulting in a furious current through the anchorage. As they huddled below, terrified by the creaking and popping of the lines, Larry and Mary thought they were goners.

As the storm progressed, radio stations went off the air one by one. At the height of the hurricane, only one local AM station was broadcasting, and Larry and Mary could hear it only intermittently. They were cut off from any help or contact with the outside world.

The eye passed directly overhead. The wind shifted 360 degrees and their boat, still held with its bow facing upriver by the tremendous current, danced on the straining anchor lines. First, the boat swung to the left, far over, almost to the shore, then as the wind shifted further, it swung back and headed off on another tack. Fortunately, the eight boats were far enough apart to avoid hitting each other while their anchors held.

Then one of the boats upstream dragged its anchors. Larry poked his head out to see if he could somehow protect his boat or help them. But nothing could be done; he could only watch as they shot by in the blink of an eye. As reported later by the Charleston *Post and Courier*, two other boaters who were anchored nearby lost their lives. Larry never learned if the boat he saw was the one carrying the doomed pair.

Eventually, the storm ended. Though they had closed every possible entry point, the cabin was mysteriously full of leaves. Up on deck, debris was plastered everywhere. But the anchors had held. Larry took some bearings, and as far as he could tell the anchors hadn't dragged a foot. Most of the other boats had survived, some better than others. The trees that he had hoped would shield them from the wind were gone; almost all of them had been blown down.

When the group recovered a bit, they motored downriver as far as they could, to a railroad swing bridge that was out of commission and could not be opened. There, they waited for weeks until electricity was restored and the bridge was repaired, allowing boat traffic to pass. Larry and Mary had to return home to children and jobs, but they left their generator for others to use.

"Since then," says Larry, "we've been through some more storms, but nothing like Hugo. Each time, preparations were a lot of work for storms that didn't materialize. But who knows when the next one will hit?"

I asked him what he would do differently next time.

As he spoke, Larry became very serious. "I would never do that again. We shouldn't have stayed on the boat. Nothing is worth what we went through. I can't tell you how many times I thought we were goners. I would never, never stay on the boat again. I'd start getting ready sooner, maybe even 3 days beforehand. There is always more to do than you realize. After Hugo, I started putting out three bow anchors not just two. I learned more about windage and what to remove and how to close up the boat more efficiently. But I would never stay on a boat in a hurricane again, never."

ON BOARD AT THE DOCK

Anthony Morrison, a commercial shrimper in the Charleston area, rode out Hurricane Hugo at the dock. He doubled up his lines and put out all the fenders and tires that he could find. In past storms, he had seen other boats slam so hard against the dock that they burst their seams so his plan was to run the engine in order to keep the boat off the dock.

The power went out early, and the only light Anthony had was the boat's searchlight. As the tide and wind increased, even he, an experienced waterman, became alarmed. Through the rain, he saw water rushing through the seafood shed 50 feet away. As the storm slammed into him, he ran the engines at full throttle to keep the boat in place at the dock and to keep the long docking lines from snapping.

During the 20-minute eye lull, he found one of his four spring lines had broken and replaced it.

When the wind returned, now from the opposite direction, it pushed the boat backward. To see better, he opened the door to the pilot house and the wind tore the door off the hinges. Water continued to rise until it was 2 feet over the pilings. For 6 hours, he stayed at the wheel, running the engine for all it was worth to keep the boat from pounding on the dock.

At daylight, the wind began to die down, and Anthony saw Hugo's destruction all around him. The 19-foot storm surge had torn three shrimp boats loose and sunk them in the creek. Docks were in the marsh, and the seafood shed was full of water. Exhausted, he walked away, telling everyone he'd never stay on the boat again.

TRUST YOUR PREPARATIONS

Story after story proves that a hurricane is nothing to fool with. Not one person I spoke to said they would ever stay on a boat in a hurricane. Some, like Anthony Morrison and the Bramletts, tried, and though they survived, they will never do it again.

Once your boat has been stormproofed, there is nothing more for you to do but go home and wait. Try to forget the boat.

Don't take that as an opportunity to go sightseeing, however. Long ago, I made the mistake of going to a beach on Cape Cod, Massachusetts, to see a hurricane's windswept waves. Within minutes of my arrival, winds of 105 miles per hour hit the shore and drove me back to the car with airborne sand pelting me all the way. As I attempted to drive to the safety of my house, I found trees and wires were down. Roads were flooded, and some were barely passable. While I had been out sightseeing, a door had blown open at home, soaking the rug and living room furniture. A frightened house cat had escaped and was lost for hours as she trembled under a bush.

Knowing that you have done all you can for your boat and family puts you far ahead of those who have remained complacent and done nothing except wait and watch. You've executed a well-thought-out plan. You've kept track of the weather advisories and so have a good idea of what to expect. You've made an early decision of whether to move your family farther inland or to stay at home with enough supplies for at least 3 days. You've kept in touch with distant family who are worried about you and yours. Now wait. It will pass and all will probably be okay. If there is such a thing as peace of mind in the face of a hurricane, you have earned it. You, your boat, and your family should come through just fine.

Appendix A:
Weather Websites

WORLD AND NATIONAL WEATHER

National Oceanic and Atmospheric Administration (NOAA):

Geostationary Satellite Server, www.goes.noaa.gov

National Hurricane Center, www.nhc.noaa.gov

National Weather Service, Interactive Weather Information Network,
http://iwin.nws.noaa.gov

NOAA Satellite and Information Service, Operational Significant Event
Imagery, www.osei.noaa.gov

National Data Buoy Center, www.ndbc.noaa.gov

University of Hawaii, Tropical Storms, Worldwide,
www.solar.ifa.hawaii.edu/tropical

The Weather Underground, www.wunderground.com/tropical

Unisys Weather, www.weather.unisys.com/hurricane

Intellicast Weather, www.intellicast.com

Caribbean Weather Information, www.caribwx.com

Tropical Ecosystems (by R. Hays Cummins), http://jrscience.wcp.muohio.edu

University of Wisconsin Cooperative Institute for Meteorological Satellite
Studies, http://cimss.ssec.wisc.edu

Crown Weather Services, www.crownweather.com

Southern Regional Climate Center, www.srcc.lsu.edu

Local Weather

National Weather Service, Southern Region Headquarters, www.srh.noaa.gov

Accuweather, www.accuweather.com

The Weather Underground, www.wunderground.com

National Ocean Service, Center for Operational Oceanographic Products and
   Services (tide predictions), www.tidesandcurrents.noaa.gov

For Weather Buffs

University College London, Seasonal Weather Forecasts,
   http://forecast.mssl.ucl.ac.uk
U.S. Geological Survey, Center for Coastal & Watershed Studies,
   http://coastal.er.usgs.gov
Federal Emergency Management Agency, www.fema.gov
National Aeronautics and Space Administration (NASA), www.nasa.gov
U.S. Army Corps of Engineers, www.usace.army.mil

Earthquakes

U.S. Geological Survey, Earthquake Hazards Program, 24-Hour Aftershock
   Forecast Map, http://pasadena.wr.usgs.gov/step
U.S. Geological Survey, Earthquake Hazards Program, Northern California,
   http://quake.wr.usgs.gov

Appendix B:
Hurricane Preparedness Checklist

I've adapted the following from a plan developed by FEMA and the U.S. Coast Guard.

Before Hurricane Season

- Have you made a storm preparedness plan?
- Is it posted at home and on the boat?
- Does your marina have a copy?
- Does your plan have sufficient time built in for completion before the storm?
- Have you followed a preseason equipment checklist?
- Do you know the preparation status of all neighboring boats (360 degrees)?
- Have your neighbors filed a storm preparedness plan?
- Do you have a relief skipper who is prepared to stand in in your absence?
- Are all power and electric gear in working order?
- Are all batteries charged?
- Are all lights operable?
- Have all cleats and chocks been checked for adequate backing and position?
- Are full sets of chafe gear stored and labeled?
- Do you have sufficient line for two pendants if mooring?
- Has your mooring been inspected within the last 6 months?
- Do you have the proper mooring and anchor for the type of bottom?
- Is the mooring set for all likely wind velocities and directions?
- Will scope allow for all likely wind velocities and directions?

- Do you have at least two anchors of appropriate size and design for your boat with at least 300 feet of oversized rode and sufficient chain for each anchor?
- Are automatic bilge pumps of proper size and in working order?
- Are self-bailing cockpit drains clear?
- Do you know how to remove your headsail quickly?
- Do you have a location chart for all through-hulls?
- Do you have plugs?

When a Storm Watch Has Been Announced

- Have you checked all hatches to be sure they are waterproof and taped?
- Are fuel tanks shut off?
- Have you removed all rigging, sails, dodgers, canvas, and loose deck gear?
- Have you removed all ship's papers, electronics, and personal gear?
- Have you set chafe gear at all points of possible line contact?
- Have you closed all through-hulls except self-bailing drains?
- Have you removed all portable fuel and oil storage containers?
- Have you left automatic bilge pumps on and turned off all other switches?
- Have you checked the status of neighboring boats?
- Are you continually updated on what the storm is doing? Location? Top winds? Direction of movement? Time predictions of onset? Eye location? Tide height and times?
- Are you aware of the storm's quadrants?
- Are you monitoring NOAA, VHF, and FM weather at home as well as on the boat?
- In the 24 hours before the storm, are you continually updating your plan as it relates to the predicted storm direction? Plan to be off the boat at least 4 to 6 hours in advance.

Appendix C:
Seapath Yacht Club
Hurricane Policy

Once a Hurricane Watch Has Been Set for This Area

1. All vessels moored on the south side of "A" dock will be required to move. Vessels moored on the north side of "A" dock will be moved if space is available in other areas of the marina. A "good Samaritan" policy will be in force during hurricane conditions whereas vacant slips will be used gratis for owners and permanent renters forced off of "A" dock.

2. No vessels over 60 feet will be allowed to remain in the marina.

3. All canvas enclosures and headsails must be removed. Owners of those enclosures and sails removed by the marina staff will be charged a fee.

4. All mainsails and loose items must be removed or tied securely in place.

5. Vessels must be double lined. Please refer to recommended mooring procedure available at the dock house. Vessels attended by marina staff will be charged a fee for securing vessels and the cost of line.

6. It will be up to the dockmaster's discretion to allow transient boats to relocate to safer areas in the marina or be asked to leave.

7. Dock steps must be removed and stored under the clubhouse.

8. Close all seacocks. Close engine fuel valves at the tank. Shut off propane tanks at the tank. Leave extra dock lines in the cockpit. Remove electronics, insurance papers, and other valuables from your boat. Secure wind generators and remove fans if possible.

9. Dock box lids must be securely fastened to prevent them from blowing open.

10. Bicycles should be removed from under the clubhouse for the bikes' protection.

11. Dinghies stored under the clubhouse should be removed or lashed down.

Responsibilities of the Marina Staff

1. Assure the above-mentioned directives are adhered to.
2. Board up all windows and doors on dock house and clubhouse once a warning has been set for this area.
3. Move all dock house inventories to the attic.
4. Take computers, backups, and related items away from the marina.
5. Move dockhouse washer and dryer to the social room of the clubhouse.
6. Remove flags from the flagpole.
7. Make sure oil drum in dumpster area is secured and lid to the oil drum is closed.
8. Move dock carts to social room of clubhouse.
9. Move picnic area tables and benches to the social room.
10. Secure all chairs and tables on deck area and sunset deck.
11. Move courtesy car to a safe storage.
12. Hoist dinghy lift ladders with dinghy winch and secure.
13. Secure dumpster area gates.
14. Once evacuation of the beach is imminent, secure all power and water to the marina and clean out the ice cream freezer.
15. Move all electronic hardware in dock house to the attic.
16. Secure ice machines.
17. Secure inspection plates by ice machine and water supply for "A" dock.

(Approved by board of commanders, May 29, 1999, as amended.)

Appendix D:
Brewer Cove Haven Marina
Hurricane Preparation Checklist

After the devastation that hit Florida in 2004, Mike Keyworth of Brewer Cove Haven Marina in Barrington, Rhode Island, reviewed the marina's hurricane preparation checklist. Minor refinements in prestorm preparations were needed, but procedures for dealing with the aftermath of the storm needed more major revision. Much of his new plan was designed to help the marina get back in operation with the least cost and turmoil for his tenants.

Phase One—At Least 1 Month Before Storm Season

- Review plans and update as necessary.
- Review insurance coverage and limits and modify as necessary.
- Distribute preparation plan and post for employees to review.
- Brief all marina personnel on plan.
- Engage all critical employees on their personal plan for families and property and insure that their plans are in place and up to date. Confirm contact information.
- Identify teams and assign areas of responsibility, i.e. mechanic shop and all equipment, carpenters, carpentry shop, and boarding all windows, etc.
- Appoint a noncritical employee to be on call for employee's emergency out-of-facility action on the part of critical employees.
- Check emergency supplies and restock. This should include flashlights, batteries, water, duct tape, etc.
- Make vendor list for rental and leased equipment and reserve appropriate equipment. This might include temporary office trailer, generators, pumps, etc.

- Review tenant storm plans and coordinate efforts.
- Meet with local officials and inform them of plan and potential needs and cooperative efforts.
- Obtain or prepare necessary documents, such as no parking signs, caution tape, haulout spreadsheet, etc.
- Make offsite arrangements for safe storage of sensitive files, documents, and equipment such as computers and related equipment.
- Set up storm prediction process or service.

Phase Two—72 to 48 Hours Prior to Storm Event

- Set up communication center.
- Initiate hurricane warning and activate communication plans.
- Meet with all employees to set schedule and relay pertinent information.
- Notify all tenants of schedule and situation.
- Process all mail and paperwork that can be completed immediately.
- If practical, close the facility to cars and nonessential vehicles.
- Earmark supplies for marina use and isolate to avoid depletion by nonmarina personnel.
- Begin preparation of marina.

    1. Stock emergency food and water supplies.
    2. Check emergency generators, lighting, and fuel supply. Obtain additional generators, pumps, etc.
    3. Secure outdoor furniture, large signs, flags, trash cans, dock carts, fire extinguishers, antennas, shrink-wrap, temporary buildings, scaffolding, etc.
    4. Prepare boats in slips or on land.

        Remove roller furling sails.
        Remove dodgers and bimini tops.
        Begin to haul boats and move to highest ground.
        Secure dock lines, etc.

- Back up computers and store archive tapes with records to be removed.
- Initiate plans to evacuate personnel and equipment in flood-prone areas.
- Notify any suppliers to hold shipment until after the storm.
- Ensure that first-aid supplies are on hand.

- Arrange security staff and volunteer schedules.

Phase Three—48 to 24 Hours Prior to Storm ETA

- Haul and secure workboats for safekeeping.
- Track and post hurricane information.
- Maintain contact with local emergency officials.
- Ensure that marina is secured from nonessential traffic and vehicles.
- Move files and expensive equipment to elevated and protected locations.
- Implement check-in, check-out, and duty list for personnel entering and leaving.
- Coordinate status reports on hurricane position and intensities to crews, tenants, and volunteers at the marina.
- Evacuate marina if the situation warrants or if directed.

About the Author

Bill Burr has spent a good part of his life on the water, sailing and crewing on everything from Sunfish and 45-foot racing boats to 100-foot powerboats. His *Sailing Tips: 1,000 New Ways to Solve Old Problems* has been a popular source for boaters since 1989. His most recent book, *Boat Maintenance: The Essential Guide to Cleaning, Painting, and Cosmetics* continues to be a reliable source of information about marine compounds most preferred by those who use them.

After years of living on his 37-foot Jeanneau sailboat, he left the Chesapeake Bay and moved south. Now retired, he lives in Wilmington, North Carolina, in a home overlooking the Atlantic Ocean, watches the sea, and writes about the storm just over the horizon.

Index

Numbers in **bold** refer to pages with illustrations